PON

In the same series

A PONY TO CATCH
Elinore Havers

PONY SLEUTHS
Elinore Havers

PONY PAGEANT
Sylvia Scott White

By the same Author
in Crown Pony hardbacks

PONIES ACROSS THE RIVER

THE MERRY MARCH PONIES
and other titles

PONY WATCH

by

ELINORE HAVERS

LUTTERWORTH PRESS
GUILDFORD AND LONDON

First published in the Crown Pony hardback series 1968

This paperback edition first published 1975

ISBN 0 7188 2189 0

The Publishers are grateful to Miss J. Kemp of Mounters Farm, Chawton, Hampshire, for permission to take the cover photograph at her riding stable

PRINTED OFFSET LITHO AND BOUND IN GREAT BRITAIN
BY COX & WYMAN LTD
LONDON, FAKENHAM AND READING

CONTENTS

CHAPTER ONE

"BEASTLY SHEEP RUSTLERS!"

"DADDY said we might have to leave Exmoor?" Mandy said unbelievingly. "He *can't* have."

"He did. He said if he kept on having sheep stolen he wouldn't be able to go on farming," Michael said.

Mandy laid her arms on the top bar of the gate and rested her chin on them. She gazed at the view of the moor. It was a browny-green with patches of pink and mauve where the heather was just coming into bloom. It stretched away into the distance where it was a soft blue. In the field the ponies, Inky and Chipmunk, were grazing. If they left the moor they wouldn't be able to keep ponies.

"I'm going to ask him," Mandy said. She turned and ran back to the farm followed by Michael, who was her twin.

Their father, Mr. Foster, was in the yard with Skipper, the sheep dog. Mandy came straight to the point.

"Mike says you said we might have to leave here and give up farming. Did you mean it, Daddy?" she asked.

Mr. Foster looked surprised. "I was talking to Mummie. I didn't know Michael was there."

"I was in the passage hanging up my raincoat. You were in the kitchen so I couldn't help hearing," Michael explained.

"Did you really mean it, Daddy?" Mandy asked again.

"Yes," Mr. Foster admitted. "It might happen but there's a good chance against it so don't get worried."

"Have they taken some more of our sheep?" Mandy asked.

"Seventeen ewes last night. You see," their father explained, "on a very small farm like this one, we can't afford to lose many. I've had nearly half of my flock stolen so I can't count on having enough lambs born next spring to make a reasonable profit. Less wool to sell after the shearing, too."

Mandy was silent as she thought about it. Mr. Foster had only started farming last year. She knew her mother and father had thought it over for a long time before deciding that he should give up his job and rent a small farm. She knew, too, that all his savings had gone into stocking it with sheep. Their farm had a few fields and they had the right to graze a certain number of animals on the moor.

"Large farms can stand some losses," Mr. Foster went on. "They've milk to sell, and crops of corn, probably bullocks they fatten, or pigs. We've got all our eggs in one basket—sheep."

"I'll have a big farm with a dairy herd and sell milk," Michael said. He was going to farm when he grew up. "I'll grow corn and have tractors and a combine harvester."

"It takes a lot of money to start farming like that," his father told him. "And this is a moor farm, no good for a dairy herd or growing corn."

Mandy stroked Skipper's head. He was black with white on his face and brown ears. If they left the farm they'd not be able to keep Skipper or the ponies. "What can we *do*?" she burst out impatiently.

"Beastly sheep rustlers," Michael muttered. "Can't the police catch them, Dad?" he asked.

"They keep a look out, of course. I've reported last night's theft," Mr. Foster answered. "But the moor's a big bit of country and they can't patrol it all."

"If they'd watch our bit it's all we want," Mandy said.

Her father laughed and went out of the yard with Skipper at his heels. He was going to look over his sheep before going to work in the afternoon. Because the farm would not bring in any money until the end of their first year, when there would be lambs to send to market, and fleeces to sell, Mr. Foster had taken a part-time job in the nearest town.

Mandy looked at the farm house. It was the nicest house they had ever lived in. It was whitewashed and had a thatched roof. Their mother called it "higgledy-piggledy" because the rooms led out of each other without passages, and there were big cupboards and funny little windows. And there was a huge open fireplace with a little stone seat right inside it where you could sit and toast yourself on a cold day. Even the name—Pippacotts—was nice.

"It'd be horrid to have to go back to Bristol and live there," she said. Bristol—no ponies or dogs, no moor with its rippling streams and wild animals, no kittens born in the cowshed and no baby chickens. Although they'd liked it well enough when they lived there, they hadn't known Exmoor then.

Michael looked at her. "We've got to do something about it," he said. "We could patrol our bit of the moor and give the alarm if we saw the rustlers."

Mandy's face brightened. "That's a super idea. Only I don't think Mummie'd let us go out at night."

"Very early in the morning would do," Michael said. "They can't do much in the pitch dark."

Mandy picked up a ginger kitten which was playing in the sun, patting a dead leaf with its paw. "How do they rustle sheep?" she asked.

"Drive up in a lorry, round up some sheep with a dog and drive them up the ramp into the lorry, I suppose," Michael replied. "Nobody's about at night and no one would hear them right out on the moor."

"If only the sheep would stay out in the middle they'd be safe," Mandy said.

"They lie on the sheltered side of a hill," Michael explained. "That's along the Willacombe road before it gets to the village. Another bit is under the hill before you get to the bridge. Both those places are on roads that aren't used much. If we could watch there they couldn't get our sheep without us seeing them."

"Then we'd rush to the 'phone and get the police," Mandy said, cuddling the kitten under her chin where it sat purring loudly.

"Yep," Michael answered. "We'd have to go every night, I mean morning, and ride round by both those places."

Mandy put the kitten down beside its mother who was washing the tabby kitten. She was called Sooty and Mandy had named the yellow kitten Marmalade. There were two other cats and they all came to the cowshed door at milking time for their milk. The Fosters had only one cow. She was yellow and white and was called Primrose.

The twins thought about their plan for the rest of the day and at supper they told their parents about it.

"Quite a good notion," Mr. Foster said. "I've thought of doing it myself only I can't be out half the night and run the farm and do a half day's work in the town."

"We're not at school now, we've all the hols," Michael said. "We could have a bash at it."

"Chasing sheep thieves isn't a job for children," Mrs. Foster said.

"We wouldn't chase them," Michael said. "When we saw a lorry, or men and dogs, we'd dash to phone the police."

"You can't ride on the moor at night," Mr. Foster said.

"But, Dad, don't they work just as it gets light?" Michael asked. "Or they wouldn't see a thing."

"That's very early in summer," Mrs. Foster said, "and children need plenty of sleep."

"If we had some other chaps and went out in turns—" Michael began.

"That wouldn't be so bad," Mr. Foster agreed. "Who could you get?"

"Only Neil. We need two more so we can go in pairs."

"You mustn't go alone. I'd not have a minute's peace," Mrs. Foster declared.

"If you can find someone to take turns with you can try it," Mr. Foster said. "They won't stick it more than a day or two," he told his wife.

"Oh thank you, Daddy," Mandy said.

"We will stick it," said Michael determinedly. He was rather obstinate and hated to have to give up. Mandy was more easy-going. To look at they were very much alike, with brown hair and bluey-grey eyes. Mandy's hair was short so when they were wearing jeans they were hard to tell apart.

"We'll ask Neil tomorrow," said Mandy. "He may think of someone else."

Directly after breakfast the next morning the

twins caught the ponies and rode over to Barton Farm, Neil Murray's home. It was less than a mile from Pippacotts.

Mandy's pony was a black called Inkspot. He had been a Show Jumper and had won a number of prizes and cups until he had strained a tendon in a hind leg so badly that he had had to give up jumping. His owner had advertised for a good home for him with only light hacking.

Mr. Foster had had no money to spare for ponies, it was all needed to stock the farm with sheep, but the twins were longing for ponies so he had looked round for two very cheap ones.

Inky suited them because they had done very little riding and had everything to learn, so they couldn't expect to gallop or jump at first.

Chipmunk, Michael's pony, was an Exmoor who had been bought very cheaply from a neighbouring farmer whose children had outgrown him. He was twenty. Chipmunk had taught the twins more than all the books on riding which they borrowed from the Public Library. In spite of his age he was still as active as his name (a chipmunk is a kind of squirrel) and he could scramble up or down almost anywhere, but he was too old to go far or fast. He was dark brown with the fawn nose which is the mark of a true Exmoor.

Sometimes the twins wished they had ponies which could gallop and jump but they knew they were lucky to have a pony each, and they were very fond of Inky and Chipmunk.

The lane from Pippacotts joined the road leading from the moor to the village of Willacombe. They cantered on the grass beside the road until they came to a gate which prevented animals grazing on the moor from straying down the road.

"My turn," Mandy said, urging Inky up to the gate. They took turns to open the gates because it was something they both liked to practise. Chipmunk was very good at gates but Inky, having been a Show Jumper, had done no cross-country hacking. It had taken all Mandy's patience to teach him to come up to a gate correctly, to pick his way over an awkward gap in a bank, or to slither carefully down one of the steep Exmoor hills. At first he had tried to rush as if he had been in the show ring and jumping against the clock but gradually he had steadied down. Mandy had been afraid if he played up he would strain his weak tendon again.

Exmoor is a very large piece of moorland with some flat stretches; there are a great many valleys which have very steep sides and usually a stream running through. Some of the moorland is boggy and there are very few roads. The highest hill is Dunkery where, years ago, a beacon used to be lit to guide travellers in bad weather or to signal some news. A great number of wild animals live on Exmoor and there are herds of ponies belonging to farmers.

The twins found Neil Murray on the lawn in front of the house. He was doing something to his bicycle which was upside down, resting on the saddle and handlebars. When he saw them, he said "Hi there!" and came to meet them.

As usual Mandy came straight to the point. "Has your father had any sheep taken by rustlers?"

"A few I think," Neil answered. "Why?"

"Daddy's lost about half his flock," Mandy replied and she told him all about it.

"Gosh, that's tough!" Neil said when she had finished. "You can't leave Pippacotts. Somebody must do something."

"The police can't guard the whole moor," Michael said. "But we could watch our bit." He told Neil their plan.

"Will you help?" Mandy asked. "Do you think we could?"

"Sure thing. Dead easy! Just ride round and catch 'em at it." Neil was always very enthusiastic about any new scheme.

"Good!" Mandy said. Mrs. Foster approved of Neil. She said he was reliable, he was older than the twins too, and if Neil was in it she was more likely to let them do it.

"Can you think of any other bod?" Michael asked. "We want four, so we can go out in pairs alternate mornings."

Neil shook his head. "No one near enough with a pony. We couldn't get about fast enough on foot. I'll do it on my own."

"There might be more than one gang," Michael said.

"If we get one lot copped the others'll clear off,"

Neil said. "Dad had some sheep taken last month. He was pretty mad but this is a big farm so it's not so serious. We've a lot of bullocks fattening and Dad goes in for pigs."

"Daddy just has sheep till he gets started," Michael said.

"Will you be allowed to go out watching by yourself?" Mandy asked.

Neil grinned. "It'll be okay. I'll just say I'm going out riding early. I do sometimes, not that early though. Anyway, Mum never minds anything."

Fine to have a mum who didn't mind anything, Mandy thought, though of course Mummie was much nicer than Mrs. Murray.

"Daddy says they won't come again for a bit and it'd be a waste of time watching for them," Michael said. "Shall we start next week?"

"Okay," Neil agreed. "It'll do Sinbad good to get some regular exercise. I want to hunt him as soon as the Stag Hunting starts. Dad's got a new hunter he's going to hunt at the Opening Meet."

Mandy and Michael weren't interested in hunting. Mandy thought it cruel (and Inky's leg wouldn't have stood up to it), and Michael, though he'd have liked to have tried it, had been told that Chipmunk was very keen with hounds, even at twenty, and that he would never hold him.

They planned when they would start watching for the rustlers and where they would go and then the twins went home.

It wouldn't be easy to catch rustlers at work, Mandy thought, as they went along beside the road over the moor, but it was worth trying. She watched Michael and Chipmunk open the gate. Inky wasn't as good as Chippy yet. If they left the moor she wouldn't have Inky. They'd *got* to stay.

"We *must* catch the rustlers," Michael said. The twins often said or thought the same thing at the same moment.

Mandy looked round at the moor which was pink with heather, and at some ponies grazing near by. They weren't wild for they belonged to a farmer and every autumn they were brought down off the moor and driven into a big yard. The youngsters would be kept and sold while the rest of the herd went back to the moor. In winter they were fed. Mr. Foster had said they would have a herd of ponies one day. Mandy was longing for this because ponies are so much nicer than sheep. It would be dreadful to have to leave Pippacotts.

CHAPTER TWO

A RESCUE ON THE MOOR

IN the afternoon the twins went for a ride on the moor. Mr. Foster had made two rules about their riding. First, that they should tell him or Mrs. Foster in which direction they were going, and secondly, that they should turn back the instant the weather looked like changing to rain. Mists blow up suddenly on moors and even people who know the way can get lost.

They told their mother they were going to Secret Coombe. This was their own name for a little valley where the short trees grew so thickly it looked too dense to get into. It was through Skipper chasing a rabbit that the twins had found a little path leading down into the tiny valley.

A stream ran through it, rushing over boulders and making little waterfalls, and fish lay in the pools. Above, the trees met overhead so it was like a huge green room. Ferns grew on the steep sides, soft cushions of moss covered the stones and lichen hung on the trees like green hair.

The best of Secret Coombe was the number of wild animals they saw there. Something new and exciting was always appearing.

The stream, too, was full of interesting water

insects—caddis fly making comic little houses and presently hatching out) and water-boatmen whose legs look like pairs of oars.

They had nearly reached Secret Coombe when it seemed to Mandy that the afternoon was cooler.

"I don't think I'll paddle, it won't be very warm," she said. They had built a dam across the stream to make the largest pool deeper. Even on very hot days the water was cold.

"Perhaps we'll see a dipper," said Michael. Dippers are exciting birds to watch because they go under the water and walk on the bottom of a pool.

"It's got colder since we started," Mandy remarked and glanced over her shoulder. Then she pulled up. "We ought to go back. It looks as if a mist's coming."

Michael turned in his saddle. "Bother! It does look like it." He turned Chipmunk, Mandy turned Inky and they began to trot back towards Pippacotts.

They met the breeze which was cold enough to make them wish they were wearing jerseys over their T-shirts.

"It does change so quickly," Mandy said rather crossly, "it was lovely this morning."

They cantered up a long slope and from the top they saw a great bank of grey mist rolling towards them.

"Here it comes," Michael said. "I knew it would." He sounded quite pleased.

"We'll soon be home," Mandy said cheerfully. "We've not come far." They trotted along a grass track. There were banks of heather on each side. The ground was soft and dark, almost black, and peaty. Now they couldn't see far ahead and in a few minutes the mist was upon them, like a white curtain, and they could only see a few yards in any direction.

"We've only got to stick to the track and it'll take us home," Michael said. It wasn't the first time they'd been caught in a mist, always they'd been fairly close to Pippacotts and had followed a track or path home.

"The ponies would find their way back," Mandy replied.

The mist was damp and clammy, drops of moisture formed on the children's hair and on the ponies' ears and manes. They rode in single file with Michael leading.

"We mustn't lose the track," he said, "where the grass is short it's jolly hard to see it."

"The ponies know the way," Mandy said again. "I bet Chippy'd find his way in the thickest mist, as he's always lived on the moor. But I don't suppose Inky could."

"We're okay," Michael said confidently. "This is the track all right."

Then Mandy pulled up. "Did you hear that, Mike?"

He stopped too. "No. What was it?"

They listened but they heard nothing. No larks

were singing now, or curlews whistling. The cold little breeze chilled them and the ponies fidgeted.

"It can't have been anything," Mandy said, "but I thought I heard someone calling."

As they moved on both heard it. Someone was calling for help. A faint, rather shrill cry, someone young, Mandy thought. "It is somebody calling," she exclaimed.

"Someone lost in the mist," Michael said. He shouted "Coo-ee" and they listened.

Faintly the cry came back. "Help!"

"I knew I heard something," Mandy said triumphantly. "Where are they?" She turned Inky in the direction from which she thought the sound had come, it was confusing in the mist and hard to tell just where it was. "Over here, isn't it?"

"Yes," Michael said. "But don't go. Stop, Mandy."

"We must find whoever it is and help them."

"Of course we will. But we mustn't leave this track. We'd never find it again," Michael said. "You stay here, then you can call to me and guide me back. That way we can't get lost."

Another despairing wail came through the mist. "Hi, is there someone there? Help!"

"You go, Mike," Mandy said. "Coming," she shouted.

Michael turned Chipmunk and rode into the heather beside the track. In places it reached his feet and it was very wet. Chipmunk picked his way through it carefully. "Where are you!" Michael called. "Keep shouting."

The voice answered, "Here," it sounded stronger and no longer forlorn.

Michael called "I'm coming," as he vanished into the white blanket of mist, leaving Mandy on the track.

She listened to Chipmunk brushing through the heather and thought Chippy's very sure-footed and he won't get into a bog. Moor ponies don't, they have an instinct that warns them. Then she couldn't hear anything and the voice was silent.

Michael rode straight towards the sound of the call for help. It couldn't be far as they'd heard it clearly, and with Mandy waiting to guide him back to the track he was in no danger of getting lost, though this was the thickest mist he had ever seen. Why couldn't the person who was calling come to them, he wondered? What could have happened?

Chipmunk startled him by neighing suddenly and the next minute there was an answering whinny and a pony loomed up out of the mist. Chipmunk stopped and the other pony stretched out his neck to sniff at Chippy. Michael saw that the pony was saddled and bridled. He leaned forward and grasped one of the reins. The pony swerved away but Michael hung on. "Steady boy," he said and then called "Hey there. Where are you?"

A voice quite close to him answered "Here," and Michael rode towards it leading the riderless pony.

A small figure appeared, looking shadowy and grey in the mist. In another few steps it was close enough for Michael to see that it was a girl of about his own age. She wore jodhpurs and a yellow jersey and she looked very wet.

"Oh, you've caught him! How marvellous!" she exclaimed.

"Are you okay?" Michael asked, handing her the reins.

"Yes, thanks. I didn't come when I heard you call because I was trying to catch Whitesock. I'd nearly got him but he just dodged away. I thought if I went to where you were calling I'd never find him again. I say, do you know the way to anywhere? This mist's absolutely awful!"

"Yes, once we get back on the track we'll be okay."

The girl mounted her pony and Michael turned Chipmunk round. "This way I think. I left Mandy, my sister, there so she could yell and guide me back. Hi, Mandy!" he shouted.

"Here." Mandy's voice was further away and more to the left than he had expected. "Go on calling," he yelled.

She kept calling and they rode slowly towards her and came out on the track. Suddenly Mandy and Inky were there, quite close, yet a minute before they'd not been visible.

"It's a frightfully thick mist, I'd never have found the track again if you hadn't been here and calling out," Michael said.

"It's a jolly good thing you thought of me staying here and that we didn't both go," Mandy said. "What happened?"

"I don't know," he answered and they both looked at the girl on the pony.

"I fell off and Whitesock wouldn't let me catch him," she explained. "And then suddenly it got all foggy and when I heard you I was terribly relieved. So I shouted and I was coming to find you but I was afraid I wouldn't find Whitesock again. I nearly caught him several times. He was simply maddening!" She patted him and added, "He's not even my pony so I simply couldn't lose him."

"Where do you live?" Mandy asked.

"In London mostly, but we're staying at Southcott Farm. Mummy and I—that is, Daddy's abroad. I'm Sally Reeves. Where do you live?"

"Quite close. Pippacotts Farm."

"Can you find your way in this ghastly fog?" Sally asked.

"If we stick to this track it'll take us there. As long as we don't get off it by mistake," Michael answered. "But I think the ponies would take us home."

"I daresay Whitesock would go home to Southcott," Sally said, "as he lives there. We've hired him for the whole of the hols. Are those your own ponies?"

They told her about their ponies as they rode back to Pippacotts which turned out to be quite near. Then they escorted her as far as the road to make sure she found her way back to Southcott.

"Straight down here and turn left at the bottom of the hill just before you get to the village," Michael said. The mist was much thinner on the edge of the moor and they could see that there was none down in the valley.

"It's only about ten minutes from here," Mandy said, "could you come out riding with us some time?"

"I'd love to," Sally answered. "It'd be fun. And Mummie doesn't much like me going far alone. I must say, Exmoor's a super place, but not when there's a mist!"

"It'll soon blow over," Michael assured her hopefully.

"We'll come and find you, to go out riding," Mandy said, "one day soon."

Sally rode off down the lane and the twins went back to Pippacotts. Mrs. Foster was relieved to see them and hustled them to change their damp clothes. Tea was very welcome and warming after their chilly ride.

"It's terribly lucky we heard Sally call," Mandy said after tea, when they were cleaning their tack. They didn't do it every time they rode (though they always meant to at the beginning of every holidays) but they thought it was bad for it to be put away wet.

"She'd never have found her way," Mike agreed. "It'd be beastly to get lost all night on the moor."

"Ghastly!" Mandy agreed. "Terribly cold. And no supper. I'm glad we met her because she seemed rather decent."

"If anyone got lost there'd be a search party," said Michael, saddle-soaping his reins. "That'd be rather fun. Lots of people all riding about the moor at night, with lights."

"We'll be riding about at night, at least almost night, and without lights," Mandy said, "as soon as we start our watch for the sheep rustlers."

"We must get out there early so we don't miss 'em," Michael said. "While it's still pretty dark."

Mandy wondered if it would be a little bit frightening right out on the moor in the dark. Then she remembered that they would be working in pairs and if there's two of you you're not likely to feel lonely. And there wouldn't be anything to be scared of.

CHAPTER THREE

SECRET COOMBE

THE next morning Mandy saw at once that the mist had gone but the weather had changed for the worse. Dark clouds were blowing across the sky and by breakfast time it was raining hard.

"No riding," Mandy said disappointedly. It was too bad to have wet days in the summer holidays. Her mother asked her to help with the house-work —a thing Mandy hated—and as she dusted she kept looking out of the window to see if the rain had stopped.

By midday it had eased to a steady drizzle and after lunch Neil arrived riding an enormous grey horse. The twins rushed out into the yard without stopping to put on raincoats.

"I say, Neil! What a monster horse! Whose is it?" Michael asked.

"You look quite titchy! And miles up!" Mandy said. "How high is he?"

"Sixteen two. Dad's new hunter," Neil replied. Little streams of rain were dripping off his cap and running down his mackintosh. "Dad wouldn't let me ride him at first but I worked on him until he did. He's dead quiet."

"He's lovely. I adore greys." Mandy patted his

neck which was beautifully dappled. "What's his name?"

"Grey Goose. I ask you! Calling a horse a goose! And anyway it ought to be gander!" Neil said scornfully. "We're going to change it."

"Starlight," Mandy suggested. It was her favourite name for a horse and it suited a grey.

"Grey Bird," Michael said. "That's better than goose." He had started taking an interest in all wild life since they had come to live on Exmoor because they saw so much of it, and birds were what he liked best. Mandy liked deer and foxes but they didn't often see any.

"Not bad," Neil said. "I just came to say I'll start the watch on Tuesday, if that's okay by you?"

At this moment Mrs. Foster called from a window that the twins were to come in out of the rain.

"Just coming," Mandy called back.

"Okay," Michael said. "We'll start on Monday. And then we'll go on doing alternate days."

"We won't be allowed to do it if this weather goes on," Mandy said suddenly. They had not thought that sometimes it would be too wet to go out and watch.

Mrs. Foster called again that they were to come in at once.

Michael said quickly, "Okay, we'll start Monday unless it's pouring. I daresay they won't come if it is."

"Dad thinks they won't come quite soon after

the last time," Neil said, "so this weather doesn't matter."

"Come in at once," Mrs. Foster called, crossly this time.

"We'll ride over to you as soon as it's fine," Michael shouted before they dashed indoors. From the porch they watched Neil ride away, looking rather small on the large horse.

"Super horse," Michael said.

"I wish Daddy had one," remarked Mandy, "He said once that he'd buy a cob to ride on the moor to see to the sheep when the farm started to pay. He likes riding."

"All the more reason for catching the rustlers," Michael said, "we're jolly well going to." He had what his mother called his "obstinate face".

"And our Exmoor ponies," Mandy said longingly. As soon as the sheep were profitable, Mr. Foster was going to buy a few Exmoors and start a herd of ponies on the moor. Mandy was longing for this to happen.

It was three days before the bad weather went away to wherever bad weather goes. The children decided it was time to start watching for the sheep thieves.

"They may come any day now," Mandy said, "Perhaps Neil won't mind going alone, he's allowed to do almost anything. And he is a bit older than we are."

"Four would be much better than three," Michael said. "We might need to separate, to get a message to Daddy or something. One alone would get in a jam."

"Sally!" Mandy exclaimed. "She might come. She's got a pony and she's near. She seemed awfully decent, as if she'd like anything exciting."

"She doesn't know us at all," Michael objected.

"We rescued her in the mist, so she should want to help us," Mandy declared. "If she's allowed to. Let's go and ask her."

They rode to Southcott Farm and found Sally grooming Whitesock. He was tied up in the shade in the yard. She was very pleased to see them and they asked her to come for a ride.

As they rode up to the moor Mandy told her about the rustlers, how important it was to catch them and their plan for patrolling.

"What super fun," Sally said, her eyes shining. "I'd love anything like that. People never have any adventures; at least I don't."

"Would you be allowed to come with us?" Mandy asked.

Sally thought about it. "I think I might be. If it wasn't going alone Mummie might let me."

"You and I could be one patrol and Mike and Neil the other," Mandy said. "Alternate days 'cos Mummie won't let us go every day. She thinks we'd be too tired."

"Mummie'll probably make me rest in the afternoon," Sally said.

"Mummie will too, if she thinks of it," Mandy said gloomily.

"I'll ask her as soon as we get back," Sally said. "Oh, I do hope she lets me. It'd be terrific fun." She slapped a horse-fly on Whitesock's neck. "Where're we going!"

"Secret Coombe," Mandy told her. "That's our name for it as it's too small to have a proper name. It's a super place, and marvellous for seeing wild animals. Once we saw a fox quite close. And a badger, but we only got a glimpse of him."

"The moor's the most wonderful place," Sally said. "You are lucky to live here."

"It'd be awful to have to leave it," Mandy replied. "Although when we lived in Bristol we thought it was quite nice there. Only we didn't know what Exmoor was like then."

"Do you ride a lot?" Michael asked Sally. She rode well and had smart riding-kit, jodhpurs and a yellow turtle-necked jersey, a black velvet crash cap and real jodhpur boots, besides a leather covered riding whip.

"Not nearly enough," she answered. "I have riding lessons all the term at boarding school. Daddy has to go abroad a lot so we're hardly ever in the same place for the hols but I generally find somewhere I can ride. It's terrific here, with Whitesock all to myself for the whole hols and the moor to ride on."

They cantered across to the Secret Coombe, having explained to Sally that they couldn't gallop their ponies.

"Bad luck," she said, "but it's worth putting up

with to have ponies of your own. I'd almost rather have one with only three legs than none at all!"

They rode down a track which ran slanting along the side of a hill. They crossed a little stream, splashing through the clear, amber-coloured water which babbled over stones and cut a deep channel through the peaty soil. The bracken came up to the ponies' withers at the bottom of the coombe and they turned off the track and, dismounting, led their ponies between the trees to where the little glen became wider. The branches met overhead, the sides of the coombe were steep and it seemed to Sally they were hidden from everyone outside.

"It really is a secret —" she began but Michael, who was leading, stopped and whispered, "Look."

Sally and Mandy looked where he was pointing and gasped in amazement. Only a little distance from them stood two deer—a hind with her calf. Mandy had seen red deer on the moor but never as close as this. The hind so graceful and beautiful, with her big dark eyes and glossy summer coat and the little calf, with babyish long legs and a fawn coat spotted with white, large round eyes and big ears.

For a few precious seconds the children gazed at them and the deer stared back. Then the hind, her nostrils quivering as the scent of humans reached her, turned and cantered away through the trees, her calf keeping close behind her.

"Oh, how marvellous!" Sally said. "I was

longing to see some deer and I never thought I would. Aren't they lovely and the baby one was adorable."

"They're gorgeous," Mandy said. "We've never seen any as close as that before."

"You wouldn't recognize them in the winter," Michael told Sally. "They lose their summer coats and look all ragged and they get awfully muddy. And in the autumn the stags fight; sometimes we hear them roaring. And they lose their antlers and grow new ones. I've got one at home that I found."

"We were awfully lucky to see those so close, we must have been down wind to them," Mandy said, "they have a fearfully keen sense of scent and that makes them hard to get close to. Wasn't the calf sweet?"

"I thought the young ones were called fawns," Sally said.

"Not red deer," Michael told her. "They're stags, hinds and calves. Fallow and roe deer are bucks, does and fawns; silly I call it, to have it different."

They tied the ponies under shady trees and showed Sally the dam they had made. They looked for a dipper but didn't see one and they lay beside the stream watching the trout and trying to catch one in their hands, also without success.

"It's a marvellous place, it might be your very own," Sally said, when they rode up the track towards Pippacotts. "I quite see that you don't want to have to go away and live somewhere else."

"We aren't going to," Michael said grimly.

When they reached Southcott the twins waited in the yard outside the farm house while Sally turned out Whitesock and then went indoors to find her mother.

"I do hope she'll be allowed to come with us," Mandy said anxiously, at least three times while they waited.

At last Sally reappeared bringing her mother to meet the twins. "I've told Mummie about it," she said. "Mummie, this is Mandy and that's Michael."

The twins said how-do-you-do and Mandy, who always went straight to the point, asked Mrs. Reeves if Sally could come with them early in the mornings.

Mrs. Reeves, who was wearing very smart dark green slacks and a leather jerkin to match, smiled and said, "I'd like to know a bit more about it." She had a very nice smile and Mandy smiled back.

"I'll try and explain," she said. When she had done so Mrs. Reeves looked at Sally. "I suppose you want to, Pet?"

"Terribly badly. Please, Mummie."

"I don't see that you can come to any harm, if you're together," Mrs. Reeves said thoughtfully. "No trying to tackle the thieves, mind."

"Oh no, we don't mean to let them see us," Michael explained, "we just want to give the alarm so Daddy can get the police."

"And your parents are quite happy about you doing it?" asked Mrs. Reeves.

"We had a job to persuade Mummie," Mandy admitted. "But Daddy said it'd be okay so Mummie said we could, if we only go alternate mornings, and not when it's dark or if it's raining."

"That sounds reasonable," Mrs. Reeves smiled. "All right, Sally, you can try it. But you must give it up if you get very tired, Pet. Better have a little rest after lunch."

Sally groaned. "I hate resting. But thank you most awfully, Mummie. It'll be terrific! When do we start? Tomorrow? And where do we meet?"

"Just up the lane," Mandy said. "Come back with us and I'll show you. You and I go together and Mike goes with Neil. I say, I hope the girls get the rustlers caught."

Michael snorted scornfully. "You'll never wake up in time."

"Have you got an alarm clock, Sally?" Mandy asked.

Sally said she'd borrow one. The twins said goodbye to Mrs. Reeves and they showed Sally where to meet Mandy the next morning at four o'clock.

"Patrolling's beginning," Mandy said.

CHAPTER FOUR

THE FIRST WATCH

THE alarm clock went off with a loud, jangling noise and Mandy woke at once. She was going out to watch for the rustlers. Exciting! Fun! Of course they wouldn't catch them the first morning but they would one day. Or one night—she thought, noticing that outside it was still quite dark. She'd set the alarm for a quarter to four.

Pulling on jeans and a thick jersey (Neil had said wear dark ones so they wouldn't show up) didn't take more than three minutes. There was no point in washing as she was sure to get grubby and to have to wash before breakfast. So she was downstairs five minutes after the alarm had gone off.

Mrs. Foster had said they must have something to eat before going out and she had left a glass of milk and a slice of cake all ready. Mandy ate it beside the kitchen stove which was pleasantly warm to lean against. Primrose's milk was much the nicest she had ever tasted and she tilted her head back and rested the rim of the glass on her nose so as to get the last drop. It felt rather strange to be up, drinking milk and eating cake, when everyone else was asleep upstairs.

Unbolting the back door she went out. The sky

was a pale grey with a few tired-looking stars which had nearly disappeared. It was rather cold and a chilly breeze ruffled Mandy's hair. Skipper came out of his kennel, his chain jingling, and whined hopefully.

"I can't take you," Mandy said, "sorry, Skip boy!" She patted him and he went back to bed.

The twins had brought both ponies in the night before, thinking that if Chipmunk were left alone he might try to break out of the field, especially as Inky would probably neigh to him.

The stable had originally been stalls but Mr. Foster had pulled down partitions and made two loose boxes. One stall was left and it was a handy place to hang their tack and keep their grooming kit, and a supply of hay and bedding.

It was pitch dark inside the stable but Michael had thought of this and lent Mandy his cycle lamp. Unfortunately the battery was nearly finished so it only gave a feeble light but it was better than nothing and Mandy saddled and bridled Inky quite quickly.

Chipmunk neighed anxiously when she led Inky out. She hoped he wouldn't go on neighing and wake her father and mother for she had a feeling that it wouldn't take much to make her parents stop them going out early.

Everything looked grey and blurred so it was quite difficult to distinguish anything until you came right up to it, but it was getting lighter every minute.

There was something wonderful about being out so early, the air was gloriously fresh and Mandy had a feeling of freedom. She wished Michael was with her. It was well worth getting up early—and if they caught the rustlers at work! What a triumph it would be!

By the time Mandy reached the gate on the edge of the moor Chipmunk's neighs had died away. As she came near the meeting place Inky began to step out a little faster and then he whinnied softly. There was an answering nicker and Mandy knew Sally was near. But she didn't see her at first. She was under some trees and she didn't show up at all, neither did Whitesock who was a very dark brown Exmoor.

"Gosh! You're almost invisible!" Mandy said as she rode up. "I couldn't see you till just now."

"I've got black jeans and a black jersey. A super thick one. I made Mummie buy me some yesterday, so I needn't put on jodhs every time I ride. We got black ones as they won't show up. The only bit of light colour on us is Whitesock's white sock."

Mrs. Reeves must be quite rich, Mandy thought, as they rode back together, for her mother never bought the twins clothes unless they really needed them.

"Isn't this exciting!" Sally was saying. "I'm thrilled to bits!"

"Same here. If only we see them and get them caught."

"We will sooner or later," Sally said confidently.

"As long as we're allowed to keep on doing this watching."

"Daddy said we wouldn't stick to it," Mandy said. "I think that helped to make Mummie let us; she thought it'd only be for one or two mornings. But Mike's most frightfully obstinate and he wouldn't let us give up, even if we wanted to."

It was cold enough still for them to be glad of their thick jerseys. When they came to the gate Inky was tiresome about opening it and not to waste time Mandy let Sally do it. Whitesock was good at gates. "Better than I am," Sally said, "as I've not ridden about in the country much, mostly at riding schools or for dull rides along roads. I say, Mandy, I could meet you at the gate another morning. It'd save you coming down the hill."

"Could you! That'd be marvellous. Mike and I thought you might not want to come so far on your own."

"I don't mind," Sally said. "Where are we going to do our watching?"

"Our bit of moor, where our sheep graze most, is between the two roads. At least it's the same road only it does a loop down into Willacombe. Daddy says it's why he loses sheep, because they're always near a road."

"I shouldn't have thought anyone could catch sheep out on a moor."

"It's fairly easy, with a sheep dog or two. And there's never anybody about right out here in the middle of the moor, not at this time."

"It's getting light," said Sally. "We ought really to get up a little bit earlier so as to be out before daylight begins."

"It'll be later every morning," Mandy pointed out. "So if we stick to the same time we'll be okay."

A high bank with bushes growing on the top was on one side of the path and on the other side was the moor. Soon the bank turned away from the path and went downhill, it formed the fence of a small field. They had reached the road where it came up from Willacombe (the lane from Pippacotts joined it much lower down). Beyond the road the moor stretched away for miles. It was dark grey against the paler sky which was streaked with layers of silvery clouds.

They drew up and gazed across the moor. The sky and the moor both seemed very large. The sun was beginning to come up and to edge the clouds with gold.

Mandy looked up and down the road. There was nothing to be seen; nor anything to be heard. Absolute silence—there couldn't be any rustlers about, sheep on the move always bleated and dogs always barked.

"Nothing doing!" she said. "Let's go on to the other road."

"Where does this one go?" Sally asked.

"It goes down into Willacombe, our lane joins it, but you know that, of course, the other way it goes across a corner of the moor and joins a main road," Mandy explained. "When it comes up from Willacombe, a good way further on from here, it crosses another bit of the moor and joins a different road. The bit in between is like a huge U. That's where our sheep graze mostly."

"Not in fields?" Sally asked.

"On the moor in summer. The fields are made into hay," Mandy answered. "I expect Daddy will keep them in fields most of the winter, nearer the farm for feeding them and looking after them. Specially when they're lambing. Only we haven't many fields."

"Look," Sally pointed to where half a dozen sheep were lying in the heather. "Nobody can have been here tonight or they wouldn't be sleeping peacefully."

"I didn't think we'd see the rustlers the very first time," Mandy said.

"Why are they called rustlers?" Sally asked.

"I haven't a clue. No wonder they get caught," Mandy said, "we came right up to them, or we'd not have seen them in this half-light, and they didn't move. Let's go to the other road." She turned Inky and crossed the road. They took a narrow path between clumps of gorse and little stunted trees. Then they came out on the open moor and the track went on, grassy and smooth with heather on each side. It was getting quite light now.

"I've never smelt anything so heavenly," Sally said, "heathery and gorsey and peaty, all mixed up! Shall we canter?"

"Better not," Mandy answered. "We've got to be careful. The other bit of road's just over this little hill. If we dash up to it and anyone was there we'd have had it."

"Okay, let's go on our hands and knees!" Sally said laughing.

She was great fun, Mandy thought, really terribly nice and it was a bit of luck getting to know her.

"Neil said one of us ought to hold the ponies while the other one scouted, in case the rustlers were near the other side of the hill," Mandy said.

"You do the scouting today," said Sally. "I'll do it next time. I bet we'll have to do this simply hundreds of mornings before we find them."

"Okay." Mandy dismounted and gave Inky's reins to Sally. "Neil said we mustn't show up against the sky line, so I'll scout on foot from here."

"Do your Red Indian stuff!" Sally said.

Mandy laughed and then went up the slight slope. It was light now and the sky ahead of them was a pale yellow, the hill top looked dark against it. Mandy went forward cautiously, stooping and keeping her head down. When she was almost at the crest of the rise she went on her hands and knees and crawled until she could see over it. Then she lay flat and peeped over. Of course there wouldn't be anyone there!

CHAPTER FIVE

ON THE TRAIL

THE wide expanse of moor looked very peaceful in the soft light of dawn. The clumps of trees were dark and the steep valleys looked shadowy. Mandy lay on her tummy with her chin on her hands and thought it was very beautiful. The light in the east was getting stronger every minute. The sun's just going to come up, Mandy thought, it'll be rather super to see it actually come over the horizon.

She looked across the heathery moor. On it were deer, foxes and badgers, besides all the little rabbits, weasels and field mice; they'd all be going into shelter now after hunting and feeding in the night. She looked carefully, from one side to the other, hoping to see some deer or ponies. Ponies weren't really wild animals but they were very nice.

Suddenly somcthing caught her attention. Something was glittering and winking. Water? No, there was no pool over there. It was sunlight on a car. She glanced up and found that the sun was shining. Bother! She'd missed seeing it come up.

She looked back at the clump of trees which hid something. A car—no, it was larger than a car, she could make out the roof although it was partly hidden by leaves—it was a lorry.

Mandy's heart began to beat a little faster with excitement. What was a lorry doing hidden under trees? It wasn't far from the road, the ground there was fairly level and, at this time of year, dry enough for anything to drive across it without becoming stuck. But why was it there? It must be the rustlers! The very first morning too!

She slid back from the ridge and then ran, carefully keeping her head down, to where Sally waited with the ponies.

"See anything?" Sally asked.

"Yes. A lorry. Sally, it must be them."

Sally gasped. "Honestly? Where?"

"It's hidden under some trees," Mandy told her. "I can't think what it's doing. It's quite light now so you'd think they'd have gone, and not still be hanging round."

She was mounting Inky as she spoke and she turned him back towards the way they'd come.

"What are we going to do?" Sally asked, turning Whitesock to follow Mandy and Inky.

"We've got to get the lorry's number. It's not far away but we'll have to go round so as not to be seen. We'll have to hurry in case they go."

"I say, how exciting!" Sally dug her heels into Whitesock to make him trot faster. "But shouldn't we phone the police?"

"We must make sure they're taking sheep," Mandy said. "We'd look pretty silly if they were just ordinary people who'd broken down or something. Besides, if we give a false alarm the police wouldn't come another time, when we'd really got the rustlers."

"I hadn't thought of that," Sally said. "We must make sure. Oh, I do hope we can get their number."

Mandy was trying to work out the best way to where the lorry was hidden. To reach it without being seen they would have to ride in a half-circle keeping on low ground so that there was always a hill between them and the lorry.

"It must be them," she said, "who else would hide a lorry out here at four o'clock in the morning?"

"It's bound to be them," Sally agreed, "but we must make sure. Only they may be gone when we get there."

"We can't go fast," Mandy said, "it's not only Inky's leg but it's too rough to bat along. But we're on the trail!"

"You couldn't ride up and down those hills," Sally said, looking at the steep sides of the coombe they were riding through. "Absolute precipices!"

"People do," Mandy told her, "people who are used to Exmoor and on horses who know it. The man we got Chipmunk from said he'd gallop up and down anywhere safely, as long as he had his head and was left alone. When he was hunted he was frightfully keen and hardly anyone could hold him. I bet Whitesock could go anywhere as he's an Exmoor."

They had come to the end of the coombe and it began to widen out and to turn away right-handed. On the left a path zig-zagged up on to the high, flat moorland.

Mandy slipped off Inky and led him up. "Scrambling up a steep place might strain his hind leg," she explained, "it's less risky with no weight on his back. It's a nuisance having to remember about it always, but I can't let darling Inky break down."

At the top she halted and Inky took the opportunity to snatch some grass. Mandy looked carefully but they were not yet in sight of the trees where the lorry was hidden.

"Okay," she said, putting her foot in the stirrup. "We can canter across here," she added, as she swung herself into the saddle. "Only we'll have to be careful when we get close."

"But does it matter if they see us?" Sally asked. "We could be just out for a ride rather early. And they can't be stealing sheep now it's light."

"I don't know," Mandy said slowly. "It's odd. Perhaps something delayed them. It'd be better if they didn't see us. If they recognize us another time they might guess we were watching for them and be scared off."

"I don't want to be recognized by thieves," Sally exclaimed. "I'd be scared."

"Steady here." Mandy drew Inky back to a walk. They were coming out on a flat stretch of moor with no cover.

"From here we'll be able to see the place where

the lorry is," Mandy went on. "That clump of little trees—do you see—" she pointed.

"Those straight ahead?" Sally asked. "I can't see any lorry."

"It's hidden by all the leaves. Probably we shan't see it till we get close, not from this side. I could only see a bit of it from up on the hill. The road's just beyond it."

"Are we going to ride up to it?" Sally asked.

"Suppose we tie the ponies to a tree somewhere near," Mandy suggested, "and then slink through the bracken. It's awfully high and it'd be easy to keep out of sight."

"Okay," Sally agreed. "Where's a good tree?"

"That one," Mandy said, pointing to a low coppice-oak nearby.

They tied the ponies up by the reins as securely as they could. Reins aren't the best things for this, they come loose easily.

"I hope they don't get away," Sally said. "Whitesock can be absolutely maddening to catch."

"And probably break a rein," Mandy said. "But we shan't be long. We've only got to get near enough to see if there's anyone there and what they're doing. And get the number."

"There's no danger if we don't actually catch them stealing sheep," Sally said rather doubtfully.

"Of course not," Mandy said cheerfully, though she didn't feel any braver than Sally.

They left the ponies, with some misgivings, in case they got hung up in their reins, or broke loose, or did something quite unforeseen, and hurried up on to the track leading to the road.

The bracken on either side was nearly as high as their heads and Mandy was thinking that it would be easy to creep up to the lorry when Sally said sharply "Hear that?"

They listened. A car was grinding along in low gear not far away.

"It's them. We must see—quick!" Mandy ran and Sally followed her. They tore along at top speed and came out beside a road. Mandy looked and saw a lorry driving away from them. "We've missed them," she said disappointedly. "And we didn't get the number."

"How sickening! But they're sure to come again," Sally said, "and we'll be ready!"

"They went to the main road, not to Willacombe," Mandy said. "I wonder where they came from."

They went back to the ponies and were just in time to stop Whitesock getting loose.

"We ought to bring halters," Mandy said, "for tying them up with."

"It's rather a good show, our having seen the rustlers already," Sally said, as they rode back. "It must have been them."

"Must have," agreed Mandy.

"The ponies haven't done much really, it'll be okay to ride again later, I suppose?" Sally asked.

"Oh yes," Mandy answered. "Even Chippy and Inky who only do light work could do masses more today. Chippy could really do a long day but he's been worked hard all his life, riding and hunting and pulling a cart, and Daddy says he'll last us till we outgrow him if we take special care of him. Besides, he's earned an easy time in his old age. It's horrid to think of getting too big for your pony."

They parted at the top of the hill. Sally rode down to Southcott and Mandy went home. Michael was in the yard. "Hello!" he shouted. "How did it go?"

"We saw a lorry," Mandy said dramatically.

"Honestly? No kidding?" Michael fairly gasped.

"It was hidden under some trees. Bring Chipmunk and we'll turn them both out. I'll tell you about it."

"We'll want them again later, most likely," Michael said.

"We can catch them. They hate being in for long."

They rode the ponies bareback to the field and as they walked back Mandy told Michael the full story.

"It jolly well must've been rustlers," he said. "I wonder how many sheep they got away with. I hope Daddy hasn't lost any more."

"It shows it's worth watching for them," Mandy said. "Only I can't think what they were doing, waiting about when it was light. Four o'clock's hardly early enough to start, it got light before we'd gone far."

"But they were still there," Michael pointed out. "And it gets darker each morning. Neil and I will be on the job tomorrow. Super!"

"Is it brekky time?" Mandy asked.

"No. Mum's still milking."

"It seems ages since I got up and I'm frightfully hungry," Mandy said. They went indoors and found their father getting Skipper's breakfast ready.

"Well, how did the Pony Watch work?" he asked.

"Pony Watch?" said Michael. "We're watching sheep not ponies, Dad!"

"You're keeping watch on ponies so it's a Pony Watch!" Mr. Foster replied smiling. "How did it go, Mandy?"

"We saw a lorry."

Mr. Foster was very much surprised. Mandy told him the details and he said it was most suspicious. "Better luck next time!" he added.

CHAPTER SIX

"*SOMEBODY'S IN TROUBLE*"

One of the many nice things about Exmoor is its nearness to the sea. From many parts of the moor the twins could look across to blue or grey sea in the distance, and the town where Mr. Foster worked was on the coast.

On the morning of a fine day that promised to be hot, he asked the twins if they would like to spend the afternoon by the sea.

"I shall be coming home a little earlier today so I could bring you back in good time," he said, "if you like to come with me."

"Super!" said Michael.

"It'd be lovely," Mandy said. She liked the sea almost as much as the moor.

"I suppose we can't bathe?" Michael asked.

"Not as you're by yourselves," Mr. Foster answered.

"And be sensible," Mrs. Foster said, "don't go getting cut off by the tide or anything silly."

They promised to be sensible and Mrs. Foster said she would give them their tea to take so they could picnic on the beach.

Directly after their midday meal Mr. Foster left to go to work and the twins went with him.

Their car was a very old station wagon. Michael often wished they had a new and posh one but Mr. Foster said theirs was much more useful on a farm.

When they came in sight of the sea it looked a silvery blue as it sparkled in the sunshine. They drove down a long hill into the small town and Mr. Foster set them down on the sea front.

"Meet me here at half past five," he said. "Have a good time. Sure you'll be all right?"

"Rather!" Michael said.

"Of course we shall be," said Mandy.

Mr. Foster drove on and the twins leaned on some railings and looked at the sea. There was a delicious, salty smell in the air and it was very hot. The tide was in and the strip of dry sand above the high tide line was crowded with people sitting in deck chairs, reading or dozing or just watching the sea. Small children were digging in the sand or filling their buckets with it. A few bathers were swimming and lots were splashing in the shallow water or just paddling.

It was the first time the twins had been allowed to come to the sea by themselves and it seemed rather strange to be able to decide what they'd do; usually their mother arranged when they should bathe and have their picnic.

"I wish we could have a swim," Michael said. "It's a pity the tide's up. It's more fun when it's low and you can walk along by the sea and find things it's left behind. And pools with crabs and shrimps are fun. There's not much to do now."

"We could paddle," Mandy suggested. "It'd be cool."

Mrs. Foster had given them each a small parcel which contained their tea. They didn't like to leave it on the sand with their sandals in case a dog took it, so they had to carry it. Michael shoved his inside his shirt and Mandy held hers under her arm. The parcels were rather a nuisance and they soon got tired of paddling.

"What shall we do now?" Michael asked as they sat on the beach to let their feet dry before putting on their sandals.

Mandy would have been quite content to sit there for a while but Michael always wanted to be doing something and he hated sitting still.

"I suppose the tide won't be out before it's time for us to go home," she said, "at least not far out."

Michael looked round. "We could go up on the cliff," he suggested. "It'd be rather super up there. I bet you can see for miles. And there're lots of gulls. I might see some new sorts of sea bird."

"Okay," Mandy agreed. She brushed dry sand off her feet and began to put on her sandals. "We could have our tea up there. It'd be nicer than here, sand always gets into it on the beach."

"We'll eat it jolly soon so we needn't carry it," Michael said.

They had a little difficulty in finding the way up to the cliffs and they spent some time looking in shop windows and choosing presents for each other.

But presently they found a steep winding path with a notice To the Cliffs. When they had toiled up it they came out on flat land where the grass was short, the ground sloped down to the cliff edge and big clumps of gorse scented the air with their sweet-smelling yellow flowers.

Looking down on the town it was all roofs, cars were like toys and people on the beach were like ants, and the bathers were just dots in the water.

"It's super up here," Michael said.

"And nice and cool," said Mandy as the sea breeze fanned her cheeks.

They followed a rough path which led along beside the cliff top. There were a few people walking, in the distance two boys were flying a kite and there were several seats where people were sitting looking at the view.

Michael stopped once or twice to look at sea-gulls. He said he was going to find out their names from his bird book when he got home.

"There must be masses of nests on these rocks," he said, "I'd like to come in the spring and look for them."

He stood at the cliff edge peering over and Mandy, who was afraid of heights, implored him not to go so close.

"It's quite okay," he said. "The edge is firm, not a bit crumbly."

They went on and the path became narrower,

the grass long and tufty and the ground uneven. There were no seats and no people admiring the view. Ahead of them they could see big woods.

"Let's have tea," Michael suggested. "Then we needn't carry it." He fished his parcel out of his shirt. It had got rather squashed and was warm.

"It's nothing like tea-time, I'm sure," Mandy said as she sat down on the grass, "but not to worry."

She undid the parcels. One contained sandwiches, some were fish paste and some were jam, the other had two large slices of cake and some biscuits.

"Mummie gave me a shilling for some lemonade or something, so we needn't carry a bottle," she said.

"We'll be jolly thirsty by the time we go back to the town," Michael said, helping himself to a sandwich. "And we mustn't be late for Daddy. The sun'll begin to go down by five," he added. Neither of the twins had a watch.

They ate slowly, looking at the sea and watching a small ship. Michael thought it was one which took visitors on trips along the coast.

"It goes to Lundy Island too," he said. "I'd love to go there, it's a super place for birds."

When they had finished their tea Mandy screwed up the paper bags and looked round for somewhere to put them. "There were some wire litter baskets further back, near those seats," she said, "but I don't see any here."

"We've come too far for those," Michael said. "I'll bury it." He found a hole and pushed it down a long way.

"Let's stay here for a bit," Mandy said, "it's awfully nice and there's no point in going any farther."

They lay on their tummies and looked at the sea. Mandy chewed a grass stalk as she thought about the rustlers. They'd been watching for over a week now but they hadn't seen anyone. Nor had they seen a lorry again. She knew that her father and mother were worried by it although they didn't discuss it in front of the children. But once or twice one of them had said something which showed they felt they couldn't go on trying to farm if they kept losing sheep.

Michael was watching the seagulls and trying to see what their markings were so he could be sure of looking up the right ones in his book.

He rolled over and looked up at the sky. It was very blue and the sun, beating down on the grass, was very hot. He felt quite drowsy. That was the worst of getting up so early. He had met Neil just before four o'clock and they'd ridden round, watching and waiting but had seen nothing. Sinbad was a smashing pony, though keen and inclined to pull, but Neil rode well.

At any rate, Michael thought sleepily, no more sheep had been taken. Daddy was worried at losing so many, though he didn't say much about it. If only they could catch the rustlers. Suddenly Michael thought of something which made him wide awake and he raised himself on his elbow.

"Full moon," he exclaimed. "We never thought of that. P'rhaps they work then. We must check it somehow."

"It'd mean going out at night," Mandy objected. "And I'm sure we wouldn't be allowed to."

"It's darker every morning, practically night at four o'clock now," Michael said. "And if they only come at full moon times we wouldn't have to go every night."

"The moon's very bright and rather red now," Mandy said. "Daddy told me it's called a harvest moon. But it's getting smaller. I noticed it yesterday evening. If it's waning it won't be full again for quite a long time."

"When it is we'll see if the rustlers come," Michael said, "But we'll go on watching till then. We've jolly well got to get them. I say, can you hear that dog barking? He's been going on for ages. And there's no house for miles."

"Rather odd," Mandy said. "If he was with somebody they'd tell him to stop. I wonder if it's a dog that's got hurt, or lost, or something. Let's go and see."

They walked a little way along the path which went between some thick gorse bushes. Then it dipped down into a deep gully which sloped to the cliff edge.

"There he is!" Michael exclaimed.

A little white terrier was standing in the path. Every now and again he gave a bark.

"What on earth is he barking for?" Mandy asked. "There's nobody with him and nothing to bark at."

The dog heard them and ran up to them. He jumped up and Mandy patted him. "Isn't he sweet! I think he's lost and that's why he's pleased to see us."

"We'll take him back to the town and tell the police," Michael said.

"If he isn't claimed we could keep him," Mandy said. "It'd be smashing to have a dog of our own."

"If Daddy let us. Only if we're going to leave Pippacotts he won't want another dog," Michael said.

Mandy didn't answer. She was thinking that it was sickening how the possibility of having to leave Pippacotts spoilt everything. "Come on, good dog," she said. "I wish we knew his name."

"He'll follow us if he's lost," Michael said.

But the dog didn't follow them. He stood with his tail drooping and a wistful look in his brown eyes when they walked away and no amount of calling would make him come. They tried all the dog's names they could think of but the dog took no notice.

"It's no use," Michael said. "We'll have to leave him."

He turned to go and the dog ran in front of them where he stood and barked.

"I wonder—" Mandy began and then the dog caught hold of her skirt and gave it a tug. After this he went back to where they had first seen him and stood there barking.

"He's trying to get us to go that way," Mandy exclaimed.

"Come on," said Michael. "I believe he wants us to help him. Someone may be in trouble."

Seeing they were coming the dog ran on ahead, stopping every now and then to look back and give an impatient bark.

"He must think we're awfully stupid, taking so long to understand what he wanted us to do," Michael said.

"Wasn't he clever," Mandy said admiringly.

"And persevering, he didn't give up," Michael said. "Nor will we, over the rustlers."

"Of course we shan't," Mandy agreed.

They followed the dog along the path, presently he went across the grass to the top of the cliff, where he stood, looking back at the twins and wagging his stumpy little tail.

"There must be somebody down there," Michael exclaimed. "Gosh, how awful!"

At that moment they both heard someone call "Help!"

"There is somebody down there," Michael said and he shouted "Coming." Then they ran to where the dog stood, went down on their knees and cautiously looked over the edge.

The cliff face was not quite sheer, it sloped

steeply down to the rocks at sea level. A short way from the top there was a narrow ledge and on this, crouching against the side of the cliff, was a little boy.

CHAPTER SEVEN

A REAL ADVENTURE

MICHAEL and Mandy knelt looking over the cliff and the dog stopped barking and stood wagging his tail.

The small boy, who looked as if he had been crying, said, "Oh, I'm so glad someone's come. I've been calling for ages. Can you help me to get up?"

"Sure, of course we can," Michael said. "You okay? Not hurt?"

"No. Only I can't climb up."

"How did you fall down?" Mandy asked.

"Jinks, he's our dog, fell down here. He was just running along and suddenly he disappeared. I couldn't reach him so I climbed down and helped him to get up. Then I found I couldn't get back."

"Hard luck!" said Michael.

"I think it was very brave of you to go down, even for a dog," Mandy said.

"It didn't look so far down. I'm not much good at climbing and when I stand up I get giddy," said the boy.

"I should too," Mandy said sympathetically. "What's your name?"

"David. What's yours?"

Mandy told him their names and patted Jinks. "He tried to tell us you were here. He kept running to the cliff and barking," she said.

"Good old Jinks! He's awfully clever," David said.

"How can we get David up?" Mandy asked Michael. "Shall we fetch someone with a rope?"

Michael looked all round. "There's not a house anywhere. It'll mean going to the town and finding the Coastguard. That'll take ages." He lowered his voice and pulled Mandy back a few steps. "I'm afraid of him falling off if he gets dizzy. We mustn't leave him. Can you go and find someone who'll help?"

"Who? The Coastguard?" Mandy asked, wondering how she would find him and if he'd come.

"I suppose so," Michael answered. "Only it doesn't really need anyone with a rope. It's such a little way down a man could reach down and help him, if he'd climb. Get somebody. I'll go down and stay with him in case he gets dizzy."

Mandy peered over the edge. The ledge looked very small for two boys. "There's not much room," she protested. "Don't, Mike. Suppose you fell."

"I shan't, it's easy, no way down at all. But *he* might if he went all giddy suddenly. If he'd stand up I could reach him, I think, but we can't risk letting him move."

Michael went to the brink again. "Got any room for me, David? I'm coming down while Mandy gets help."

David looked up and smiled. His face looked quite different, Mandy thought, he wasn't so frightened now Mike was going to be with him.

"I think there's room," David said. "Not much, though."

Mandy watched as Michael swung his legs over the cliff. She held her breath and bit her lip as he turned over on his tummy and slowly let himself down, holding on to a bush which grew out of a cleft in the rock near the top. Jinks whined and looked anxiously over the cliff edge.

"All right, Jinks," Mandy said. "They're coming back," and the little dog looked up at her and wagged his stumpy tail.

Mandy heard Michael say, "That's okay. It isn't far down. Not much room though."

"Thanks for coming," David said. "It won't be so bad now. I got scared before."

"Well, anyway the tide can't reach us," Michael said, "so there's no terrific hurry. Mandy'll take quite a long time to get to the town and back."

"We'll be late meeting Daddy," Mandy said anxiously, looking down on the tops of their heads. It really was only a very little way down to the ledge. As long as you didn't look right down to the rocks far below—no wonder poor David had felt giddy.

"I'd better go," she said reluctantly. It would be horrid to leave Mike there, and David too.

"Half a mo' before you start," Michael said. "I think we can both climb up. Miles better than sitting here." David might feel faint and fall off before I could stop him, he thought. "If you can help I think we'd do it," he added.

"Help? How?" asked Mandy.

"David can't quite reach that bush, if you lean over and get hold of his hands and pull, I'll shove."

"Is it safe?" Mandy asked. "Suppose the bush bust."

"It's absolutely firm. I felt it when I came down," he assured her. "It's growing out of a crack in the rock, not crumbly earth. The cliff edge is firm too, sloping back not overhanging. It'll be easy with a pull from you. Can you make it, David, if I help you!"

"I think so," David replied doubtfully. "I did try but I got giddy when I stood up."

"Okay," Michael said. "Let's have a bash at it."

"Mike, there's nothing for you to hold on to when you're helping David," Mandy cried, as she saw Michael standing on the ledge and helping David to his feet.

"There's a sticky-out bit of rock like a handle," he said cheerfully. "And the ledge is wider than it looks. Not to worry, Mandy. Good show, David," he added as the smaller boy stood erect. "Don't look down. Look up at Mandy. Can you reach his hands, Mandy?"

Mandy clenched her teeth. It all depended on her. She had to lean over and get first David and then Mike by the hands and help them to climb up. And she hated heights.

A long way down the sea was lazily surging on a big rock, sometimes a wave broke over it covering it with white foam. She mustn't look at it, but, face down, it was hard not to.

David was looking up at her. He looked white and frightened. It was much worse for him, Mandy thought, he was on the narrow ledge with that drop close behind him and he had to climb. She was safe on the cliff and only had to give him her hands. Besides, he was younger.

"Okay, David," she said resolutely. "Can you reach my hands? Good, got you," she went on as he gripped her. "Now."

"Take it steady," Michael advised. He had one hand on the convenient knob of rock and was holding the back of David's belt with his other.

Mandy kept a steady pull on his hands, Michael pushed under his seat and David climbed slowly up, his toes scuffling on the rock as he felt for foot holds.

His face came level with the cliff top and Mandy gritted her teeth as her arms began to ache, she wriggled back to give David room and wondered if she could hold on? She'd got to. She heaved hard and David came over the edge of the cliff and lay on the grass, his feet sticking over the edge.

"Okay now," Mandy said and he pulled himself forward and crawled away from the edge. Jinks began to jump round him and to lick his face. David caught him and stroked him and Mandy saw that he was nearly crying.

She rubbed her arms and said, "Now for Mike." She looked over the edge again and asked if he was ready.

"Yep. If I can get hold of that bush it'll be easy. But I'm heavier than David. P'r'aps I'd pull you over. Hi, David, can you hang on to Mandy's feet?"

David rubbed his eyes on his sleeve and said, "Okay." Then he took hold of Mandy's ankles, gripping them tightly.

Once again she reached over the cliff for a boy's hands. Mike's hands this time. He was stronger than David and a good climber, he'd get up easily but she was longing to see him safely on the cliff.

It was easier to reach him as he was taller but he was much heavier and there was nobody to push him, as David had been pushed. The strain on Mandy's arms was almost unbearable and for a moment she thought she was slipping forward.

"Hang on, David," she gasped and the hold on her ankles tightened and she felt him pulling against Michael's weight. She was being pulled in two, she thought, and she clenched her teeth. Her arms felt as if they were being pulled off.

Then one hand was loosed, the bush rustled violently, her other arm received a sharp tug and Michael swung himself up and then sprawled on top of her.

They scrambled back from the edge and lay panting for several minutes.

"Gosh, that was fierce!" Michael said, "tougher

than I expected. Jolly good, hanging on like that, Mandy."

She rubbed her aching arms. "I couldn't have pulled you up without David."

"Thanks most awfully," David said. "It was simply smashing of you."

He looked all right now, Mandy thought; she felt a little like crying herself now it was over. She got up saying, "We ought to go. We mustn't keep Daddy waiting."

"I must, too," David said. "My Mum'll worry."

As they walked back he told them he was staying in the town with his parents for a holiday. He'd taken Jinks for a walk on the cliff and lost him. Then he'd heard him yapping and found him on the ledge.

They parted in the town, David hurrying back to his parents, and the twins went down to the sea front. It was only just five o'clock so that they had plenty of time for orange squash, and never had it seemed so good.

Mr. Foster was astounded when they told him of their adventure. "You certainly did a good thing, plucky too," he said. "But I thought you promised Mummie to be sensible. Wouldn't it have been better to fetch help than to risk climbing up?"

"David looked so white I thought he might faint," Michael explained. "I mightn't have been able to hold him if he had. That's why I thought we'd climb. It was harder than it looked."

"Climbing often is," Mr. Foster remarked. "That's worth remembering."

"It's the first real adventure we've ever had," Mandy said. "Of course we may have another when we catch the rustlers."

CHAPTER EIGHT

MICHAEL AND CHIPMUNK

MANDY started to yawn, she tried not to but she couldn't help it. Her mother noticed and said, "You're tired, dear, this getting up early's too much for you both. I think it's time you gave it up."

"Oh *no*, Mummie!" Mandy protested. "Honestly I'm not tired, at least not very."

"I think it's sleepy sort of weather," Michael said. "That's what it is, we're not tired."

"You're both looking fagged out," Mrs. Foster said. "You've tried very hard but it hasn't been any use. You'd much better give it up now."

Mr. Foster came in just then and they began breakfast.

"I'm just telling the twins they should give up this early morning business," Mrs. Foster said, "they're looking tired from missing their sleep."

"*Please!*" Michael said. "The rustlers may come any day now. It's three weeks since we started so they're sure to come soon."

"It'd waste all our watching," Mandy said, "if we gave up and then they came at once." It'd be marvellous when they did come, she thought, and then the early morning watch would be over. No more forcing one's eyes open when the alarm rang and making oneself get up and dress. After three weeks of it Mandy heartily disliked getting up at a quarter to four, although once out on the moor it seemed worth it. The alternate mornings, when it was not her turn, were bliss but Michael said they only made it harder to get up next day.

Mr. Foster began his bacon and eggs. "They've stuck it very well," he said. "I never expected them to. Odd about that lorry you saw," he went on. "nobody lost any sheep that night. I expect the driver'd lost his way and pulled off the road to wait till daylight."

"I suppose it must have been that," Mandy said. It was a great disappointment that they had failed to take its number and that Mr. Foster's enquiries had not discovered anything about it.

"They're bound to come soon," she said (the rustlers were always "they"). "Don't make us give up now, Mummie."

"It's only because you're getting tired that I'm worried about you," her mother said.

"Carry on for a bit. Say another week," Mr. Foster said. "And then we'll think about it again."

"Oh thanks," Michael and Mandy said together.

"It's funny they've not been yet," Michael said. He began to mop up the last of his egg with a piece of bread. "I suppose they can't have got to know we're watching! If they lived near—"

Mr. Foster looked at him thoughtfully. "I hadn't thought of that," he said. "Someone local! Could be, but it's not likely. The people round here are a very decent lot. And if it was anyone living near I doubt if they'd risk it so near home, they'd be recognized too easily." He got up and pushed back his chair. "I'm going out—anyone coming as far as the gate to open it for me!"

They both went with him in the battered old station wagon as far as the gate at the top of the hill down to Willacombe, where they opened the gate and then shut it after him. " 'Bye!" they shouted. He waved and gave a little toot on the horn. They watched the car go down the hill and then started to walk home.

"Suppose we don't cop them in a week and Mummie won't let us go on with the Watch?" Mandy asked.

"It'd be simply sickening if they came as soon as we packed it in," Michael said. He kicked a stone out of the way. "I don't think Neil's keen on it any longer. He's been awfully late several mornings and he's said two or three times that it's an awful bind."

"Sally didn't turn up once last week and she's been awfully late sometimes. I went on without her and she caught me up. Whitesock's a very good pony."

"It's not important to Neil and Sally," Michael said.

Mandy sighed. The thought of having to leave Pippacotts was like a nasty cloud, distant but always there. "It's been jolly decent of Sally to come. It was fun at first but it's a bit much now. And we haven't had any good rides on the moor these hols because we've been riding early."

"We could," Michael said. "The early morning work isn't enough to tire the ponies."

"Let's ask Mummie for sandwiches and go for a long ride," Mandy said. "Not today as she's going out to some meeting in the village; we'll ask for our lunch out tomorrow."

Near Pippacotts they met Neïl on Sinbad. He shouted, "Hi, there!" When he came near he stopped and, said "I was coming to see you, Mike, about tomorrow. Can you do it? Dad and I are going to hunt."

"Okay. I'll do it," Michael said cheerfully.

Then there was a short silence and Mandy began to feel slightly uncomfortable for she guessed that Neil was going to say he didn't want to go on with their Watch. So she wasn't surprised when he said offhandedly: "I'll have to chuck it anyway."

"Oh, Neil!" she exclaimed. "They're sure to come soon, specially if we give up."

"It's a waste of what we've done if we pack it in now," Michael pointed out.

"Does Mrs. Murray say you're to stop!" Mandy asked.

"No. She doesn't really mind. She thinks we're absolutely cuckoo. Dad says it's a good idea but we'll never be in the right place at the right time."

"That's a thought," Michael agreed. He stuck out his jaw and looked obstinate. "I'm not giving up. Even if I have to do it all myself."

"You wouldn't be allowed to," Mandy said.

"I don't care. I'll go on."

"I'm not giving in," Mandy said, "not till Mummie says we must."

"Thanks for helping, Neil," Michael said. "It's more our show than anyone else's."

"That's okay," Neil said. "Sorry to chuck it, but the thing is it'll clash with hunting for the rest of the hols. It'll be super if you catch them." He turned Sinbad and as he rode away he called, "Good luck."

The twins looked at each other.

"Sally will give up too," Mandy said. "Then what!"

"Go on," Michael said doggedly. He had his "obstinate face", his jaw sticking out and a scowl like a thunder cloud.

"Mummie wouldn't let us." Mandy watched a rabbit come out of some bushes.

"We won't tell her," Michael said.

"It'd be deceitful," Mandy objected.

"I know but it can't be helped. It's in a good cause and I'm not giving in till the rustlers are copped."

It was no use arguing with Mike when he was like that and Mandy walked on in silence. Then she said, "Perhaps Sally will go on with it for a bit."

"If not I'll come so you're not alone," Michael said, "and do the days in between on my own. Mummie wouldn't mind my going alone as much as she would you."

The worst of being a girl, Mandy thought, boys were allowed to do much more. "I wouldn't mind," she said and then thought it wasn't true for she would feel a little scared at going out on the moor alone in the dark, even after all these mornings. "At least not very much," she added, because you don't pretend things to a twin. "But Mummie would worry awfully if she knew."

"You needn't," Michael assured her. "I'll come. I shall dash back and have a sleep before breakfast, there'd be a bit of time if I didn't dawdle. Mummie might let us go on if we sleep in the afternoon. Anyhow, we're going on."

"Let's muck out and get it done," Mandy said. The stables needed doing every day now that the ponies were always in at night and Mr. Foster had remarked on the amount of bedding they were using. They used bracken, cut on the moor and dried, which didn't cost any money but took a lot of Mr. Foster's time to do.

We won't be able to go on with the Watch, Mandy thought as she tossed Inky's bedding up. Mike'll get too sleepy doing it every morning if Sally gives up. She was longing to give it up herself, except for the thought of leaving Pippacotts.

The next day was fine—perfect for a picnic—and the twins set off carrying their lunch in knapsacks. Michael had done the morning patrol by himself. By hurrying he had reached home at half-past six, when he'd gone back to bed. He hadn't been able to sleep but Mrs. Foster had thought it was a good idea.

They rode over the moor past Secret Coombe and on towards a line of high ridges which Michael said were the highest part of the moor, except for Dunkery Beacon.

"If we get up on the highest bit," he said, "we'll be able to see right across to Wales. It ought to be quite clear and not hazy today. Daddy told me about it. It's further than we've ever been."

"The ponies must be very fit by now as they've had regular exercise all the hols," said Mandy. "And they're having some hay as well as grass."

They gave the ponies a small armful of hay each at night to discourage them from eating their bracken bedding. Hung up in a net it kept them busy for quite a long while.

"The hols are half gone," Michael said. "And it doesn't look as though we'll be able to stop the sheep being taken."

"Don't give up hope," Mandy said quickly. If Mike stopped believing in their efforts everything would come to an end. But she couldn't help wondering if they'd still be at Pippacotts next holidays.

Although it was warm there was a nice breeze and the flies did not trouble the ponies much.

Presently Michael said, "I'm sure it's lunch time."

"I shouldn't think it is, not yet," Mandy replied.

Neither of the twins had a watch because Michael had lost his and Mandy's hadn't gone since she forgot to take it off before having a bath. Sometimes it was rather awkward, not knowing the time.

"Well I'm hungry so let's eat," Michael urged.

They stopped by a stream and let the ponies graze while they ate their sandwiches. They didn't linger but went on as soon as they had finished eating because they had a long way to go.

They were trotting up a long, gradual incline when Michael heard something which made him turn in his saddle and look across the moor. Then he pulled up. "The hounds!" he exclaimed. "Look, Mandy!"

"It's the hunt!" she cried.

There, on the open hill slightly below them, were the hounds, a mass of black and white and tan on the light green grass. Some way behind a bunch of horsemen followed. They seemed to go slowly but they were moving across the moor at a steady pace. Michael looked ahead of the hounds to try and see the stag they were hunting but he was not in sight.

"I wonder if Neil's there," Mandy said. "I can't make him and Sinbad out. They're going to go across just ahead of us," she added.

Michael didn't answer, for Chipmunk had heard the hounds in full cry and had been fidgeting and sidling and snatching at his bit. Now he plunged forward, put his head down and went off at a gallop. Michael tried to pull him up but Chipmunk was wildly excited at hearing hounds and was determined to be with them.

He'd never known a pony could pull so hard—Chipmunk was running away. Michael clenched his teeth and tried to pull him up, sitting back and using all his weight, shouting, "Whoa"—it was all useless. Chipmunk heard the hounds he loved and he was determined to be with them. Michael's arms ached, his face was red and hot, the empty knapsack flapped on his back. Chipmunk galloped on.

He was kept too occupied to notice that the horsemen had disappeared; then suddenly he found they were at the top of a very steep hill. It was covered with patches of heather, stones and low bushes and he caught a glimpse of some riders in the coombe at the bottom. The ground seemed to drop away under Chipmunk and Michael thought, in horror, "He's going to gallop down."

"Left to themselves Exmoor ponies can go anywhere." His father's words came back to him. Michael slackened the reins to let Chipmunk have his head and sat perfectly still. They came down very fast but Michael, leaving it all to Chipmunk had time to wonder at his surefooted agility.

I'll stop him at the bottom, Michael thought, specially if they've gone up the other side, a hill like this'd stop him. But on reaching the bottom Chipmunk swung sharply and, before Michael could pull him up, he was galloping up the coombe, fighting for his head as Michael tried to stop him. They went up a long slope and came out on the moor, some way ahead were three or four horsemen, the last of the field. Chipmunk still went on.

Michael found himself enjoying it now that he'd given up struggling against Chipmunk. He'd never ridden so fast. The wind sang past his cheeks as they swung along. Super!

They raced down a long slope and Chipmunk splashed through the little stream at the bottom. Then they climbed a gently sloping incline. Michael had given up worrying, Chippy would stop when he was tiring.

At the top they found the hounds had lost the scent and checked. They were casting about while the field stood waiting at a short distance. Now we'll stop, Michael thought, as Chipmunk eased up to a canter. But at that moment the hounds got on the line again, they gave tongue, the huntsman sounded his horn, and hounds and horsemen went on. Chipmunk snatched at his bit and went off, fighting for his head.

"Oh, Chippy. You've done enough. Do stop!" Michael said in despair. They galloped on across a stretch of grass and down a long slope. All the horsemen were out of sight now. As they went up the hill on the other side Chipmunk began to slow down, his gallop became a canter, he stopped pulling and his speed slackened to a trot. He let Michael pull him up and he stopped. Michael jumped off at once.

CHAPTER NINE

TROUBLE AND A DISCOVERY

MICHAEL looked at his pony in dismay. Chipmunk's flanks were heaving fast and his breath came in sobs. His head was hanging and Michael wondered if he was going to fall down, he looked so exhausted.

He loosened his girths and then he remembered reading that a "spent" horse should face into the wind to help him to breathe. He turned Chipmunk saying, "I'm afraid you're 'spent', Chippy, and it's your own fault." He stood there, rubbing the pony's head gently and watching him. He was feeling very anxious. His arms still ached and his legs were tired. But none of that mattered if Chipmunk was all right. He was too old for this, Michael thought.

Soon Chipmunk began to breathe more slowly, his flanks no longer heaved and then he raised his head to listen.

"No, Chippy," Michael said. "You aren't going off again so don't listen for the hounds. I hope to goodness they don't come this way again."

Chipmunk seeming to have recovered, Michael decided to retrace his steps. He'd got to find Mandy who would be wondering what had happened to him. He walked so as to save Chipmunk and set off the way they'd come.

Down the hill to the little stream, where Chipmunk wanted to drink; Michael wasn't sure if he should let him, then he thought that as he wasn't very hot now it wouldn't hurt to have a short drink and it would refresh him. It was horrid to feel thirsty. Chipmunk drank noisily, and more than Michael meant him to; then he raised his head with his muzzle dripping and stood listening.

"Oh no, you don't!" Michael said. "No more hunting. You've had it, chum! Forget it!" And he crossed the stream and led him up the long hill on the other side. At the top he halted and scanned the moor. There was no sign of anyone. What a long way Chipmunk must have galloped! He had only to go back the way they'd come and he was bound to meet Mandy.

He went on, leading Chipmunk, and crossed a long stretch of moor until he came to one of the big folds in the moor with a hill slanting down it and another one on the opposite side. He went down and toiled up the far side. Still no sign of Mandy so he went on. When he came to yet another big dip, with the usual stream at the bottom, Michael thought he should have come to the steep hill by now. How many valleys did they cross? He'd been so taken up with trying to stop Chipmunk that he couldn't remember. A fear which had been lurking in his mind grew stronger.

He searched the ground for hoof marks but he couldn't see any. Of course the grass was thick and the ground firm, still, all those horses would leave some prints. There was no dodging the fact that he'd missed the way. He'd not only lost Mandy but he was lost on the moor.

Michael began to panic. Tales of people lost for a whole night came into his mind. Then he pulled himself together. Get in a flap when you're in a jam and you've had it, he told himself sternly. He couldn't be so very far from home and Mandy would go back and raise the alarm if he didn't turn up. Then he remembered that his father was working late that night—if he failed to return by supper time his mother would be terribly worried.

He'd lost all idea of direction and there was nothing but open moor on every side. Dunkery Beacon, he thought, we were riding towards it this morning. But the sun had gone in and a low bank of clouds hid the distance.

If he went on in the same direction as he'd been taking he might come to the steep hill he'd ridden down—he'd like to have another look and see if it was really such a precipice—anyway, this direction was as good as any other.

"Mandy says Exmoor ponies can find their way home," he said, speaking aloud because it seemed rather lonely on the huge moor with nobody to talk to, "so do your stuff, Chippy!" But Chipmunk was only interested in eating grass.

After walking for about a quarter of an hour he

came to the edge of a hill and looked down into the coombe. Something moving caught his eye at once. Mandy! She was riding along the valley half hidden by tall bracken.

"Mandy! Mandeee!" Michael yelled his loudest.

She stopped and looked all round. Michael waved and Mandy waved back. She started to turn Inky but he shouted "Wait" and ran down the slope with Chipmunk trotting beside him.

"What happened? Why are you leading Chippy?" Mandy called as soon as Michael came near her.

He stopped beside her. "He got away with me. He went like a bomb! I've never ridden so fast. It was super but I couldn't begin to hold him." Michael fondled Chipmunk's head. He was sniffing at Inky as if they were glad to see each other again. "Once I thought I'd stopped him, we caught up with the hunt as they'd checked, but then they got the scent again and went on and so did Chippy!"

"They said he pulled hard with hounds," Mandy said. "How did you stop in the end?"

"He was whacked. Galloped himself to a standstill. I got off and turned his head into the wind, you know."

Mandy nodded. She'd read that book too. "He seems all right now. I bet he enjoyed it. You must've gone miles. I was wondering if I'd ever find you. Actually, I was just a bit worried because I don't know the way home from here."

"Oh well, nor do I!" It didn't seem so bad now that they were together. Being lost by yourself is much worse. "Can't you find the way back that you came by?"

Mandy shook her head. "I wandered about rather, trying to find you. Now I haven't a clue where we are."

Michael thought for a minute and then said, "The best thing would be to get on a hill where we can see a long way. We might recognize something."

"Okay." Mandy turned Inky. She'd been feeling very depressed but now she was with her twin again she felt more cheerful. "Back up this coombe and we'll be fairly high up."

As they rode she asked Michael if he'd seen Neil.

"No. I hadn't much time to notice anything but I'm sure he wasn't there when they all stopped."

"He must have got left behind. Did you see the deer? I hope it wasn't the one we saw with the dear little calf."

"I didn't see it, probably miles ahead of them. And they don't hunt hinds with calves."

"Well I hope they didn't catch one," Mandy said.

They reached a high ridge and pulled up. After gazing hard in every direction they had to admit they couldn't see any landmark or bit of ground that they knew. After some discussion they kept straight on, after all, it must lead somewhere. "A farm or a road," Michael said hopefully.

Presently he noticed that tufts of grass were

growing among the heather and he remembered his father telling him that where heather and grass were mixed the ground was treacherous to ride over. He looked all round anxiously, it looked the same everywhere.

Soon after this Chipmunk floundered in soft ground, nearly shooting Michael over his head. He got off quickly and found he was ankle deep in water. He held Chipmunk's reins short under his chin and turned him back, the pony sinking to his knees and splashing as he scrambled after Michael.

"We can't go on. We must work our way round this bit."

"We didn't come across this wet bit," Mandy pointed out.

"No." Michael rubbed his chin with his riding crop. "But if you're lost on a moor you must go straight, or else you go in a circle. Let's go more to the right and keep out of this wet bit."

"I'm sure the ponies could find their way back," Mandy said, "only they don't seem to want to go home yet."

"Well we do," Michael replied. "Mummie will worry if we're very late. And Daddy's not at home so she won't know what to do."

"Let's keep on high ground so we can see a long way," Mandy suggested.

It seemed a good idea so they made for one of the long ridges ahead of them. But they were soon in trouble again. Inky floundered in a soft patch and Mandy, afraid of him straining his weak leg, jumped off and helped him to get clear. Then they came to a little stream running between banks of bright green grass. Both ponies refused to go near.

"It's a bog," Michael said, "a real deep one, not just swampy ground."

Again they went back. The ground became firmer and they trotted on, feeling encouraged. Reaching a large stream Michael proposed that they should follow it downhill. "It must go down to a river. As soon as we get off the moor we shan't be lost. Even if we're miles from home. Besides, if a mist came up we'd be absolutely done for."

So they went downhill, sometimes splashing along in the stream and sometimes riding on the bank. The water refreshed the ponies who trotted out briskly. Quite soon the stream joined another one and became too deep for the ponies and they rode beside it until they were stopped by a hedge.

"This means a field so we're getting off the moor," Michael said. "Jolly good!"

"But we shan't know where we are," Mandy said.

"We'll soon find out. People to ask. Signposts," Michael said cheerfully. "Along here," he turned away from the stream, "we'll find a gate and we're sure to get to a road soon."

The gate was in the corner of the field, down a steep hill. The ponies took it slowly and carefully. Michael said the one he galloped down was much steeper and that Chipmunk was marvellous. They went through the gate and shut it. Then they looked round and saw that the hill curved and formed a dell. A lorry was standing on the grass and three men sprawled beside it. A dog lying near them growled and one of them swore at it to shut up.

"Oh good, someone to ask the way," Michael exclaimed. He was surprised to see them there and even more surprised to notice they were playing cards. "Could you tell us the way to Willacombe, please?"

The men were watching them and looking rather unfriendly. "Where've yer come from?" one of them asked. He was a big, red-faced man wearing shabby, grey trousers and a bright blue pullover.

"Down from the moor. We got lost," Michael explained. "We want to get on to a road. And we're going to Willacombe."

The man scratched his head. "T'aint far but I dunno 'ow to tell yer. There's a gate there —" he jerked his head in the direction the lorry had come. "Takes yer on to a road, go left —"

Mandy didn't listen while the man was directing Mike because he was better at finding the way than she was. Inky moved slowly between the back of the lorry and the men, grazing as he walked. Mandy looked about her curiously. They must be spending quite a long time here for there was the remains of a meal on the grass, paper bags, several beer bottles and a thermos.

While the big man was talking to Michael she overheard one of the others mutter, "Willacombe? Ain't that where we bin going lately?" And the third man said, "Yeh, and where we'll be picking 'em up tonight."

Mandy bent forward and pretended to brush a fly off Inky's neck so that her face wouldn't show that she'd heard. Then Michael said, "Thanks a lot. Come on, Mandy, it's not far."

"Oh good!" She hauled Inky's head up, his mouth full of grass, and turned and rode past the lorry. The smell of sheep, as distinctive a smell as any, was very strong.

Michael was looking round curiously and the big man said, "We're fetching some stock from a farm, got 'ere too early so we're waiting."

"I see," said Michael. "Cheerio!" He led the way past the lorry with Mandy following him. Her thoughts were whirling round in her head. She resisted the temptation to look back and as soon as they were at a safe distance she rode up beside Michael and said, "Mike, they're the rustlers. *I know!*"

He stared at her. "How do you know?"

She began to gabble excitedly, "When you were talking to that big man one of the others said: 'Willacombe's where we've been going' and the other one: 'And where we're going to pick them up tonight.' And, Mike, the lorry smelt most awfully strongly of sheep. Horrid!"

"They do smell strong," Michael agreed. "But

any lorry could have sheep—Gosh though! it does look suspicious them saying that. It was a bit fishy what he said about them being early, of course they'd wait at the farm not in a field. It sounds feeble."

"Funny time to fetch stock surely?" Mandy asked.

"Not if they were going to a sale tomorrow, a long way off," Michael answered. "But there wouldn't be three men for that. These chaps came ready to hang about, cards and food. It's very suspicious."

"And they were rather horrid, I thought."

They reached a gate leading into a narrow, overgrown track, it twisted and turned and suddenly came out on a road. Michael looked at the ground. "Lots of tyre tracks. They come here fairly often. It's their hide-out."

Mandy was wildly excited. "They're coming tonight. We'll get them caught."

As they rode along the narrow road Michael said, "I wonder why they're here so early. I wish I knew what time they go up on the moor."

"We'll go out frightfully early tomorrow," Mandy said.

Michael looked serious. "Chippy oughtn't to be ridden again so soon. He's had a very hard day. And he's old."

"What'll we do? It's so important," Mandy said agitatedly.

"I wish Daddy was home," Michael said.

"Sally and Neil must be in on it, they'd hate to miss it," said Mandy.

"Neil won't ride Sinbad after hunting him to-day," Michael said. "Blast! Everything's going against us."

"We must have ponies tomorrow," Mandy said.

"Tell you what," Michael suggested, "we'll bike round and see Neil and Sally after supper. We can tell them how frightfully urgent it is. Neil may think of some plan."

CHAPTER TEN

"THIS IS IT!"

THEY turned the ponies out and watched them drink at the stream and then roll. "Chippy seems okay," Michael said, as the pony got to his feet and began to graze.

Going to the house, laden with their tack, Michael said, "Don't let's tell Mummie we know the rustlers are coming tonight. She'd worry. I wish Daddy was at home."

"Nicer to catch them ourselves," said Mandy. She was carrying her saddle on her head.

"Yes," Michael agreed doubtfully, for who could tell how things would turn out?

"I'm glad you're back," Mrs. Foster said when they went in to the house. She was in the kitchen and there was an appetizing smell. The table was laid too, and the twins realized that they were very hungry. "I was beginning to wonder what had happened to you."

"We went miles. We saw the hounds," Michael said.

"But Neil wasn't there," said Mandy.

"Hurry up and wash. Supper's ready. I thought you'd be hungry so I made the cheese and tomato pie that you like. And someone who ordered cream never came for it so you can have it with a tin of fruit."

"Gorgeous!" Mandy said, kissing her mother before going to wash her hands and brush her hair. Mrs. Foster made Devonshire clotted cream to sell, the family only had it on Sundays (if there was enough) so it was a treat.

Directly after the meal—which was tea and supper together in the summer holidays if they were out of doors for long—the twins got out their bicycles and went bumping down the track. They should have been helping to wash up but Mrs. Foster let them off when they said it was very important that they should see Neil.

They found him in a loose box strapping the grey.

"Hello, Neil! I say, did you hunt Sinbad today?" Michael asked.

"Yes. Why?"

"We saw them but I didn't think you were there."

"I lost them quite early. Several of us went the wrong way and came to a place we couldn't jump. When we'd gone back we'd lost them so I came home."

Michael told Neil all about Chipmunk running away and how they'd found the lorry and the three men. Neil stood leaning over the stable half-door, as he listened he looked more and more surprised.

"Crikey!" he said when Michael finished. "How smashing! Jolly good show, Mandy, spotting them. We'll get 'em this time." His brown eyes were shining with excitement, like Skipper's when he knew he was going out, Mandy thought.

"The thing is," said Michael, "I don't think I ought to ride Chippy, not after all he did today."

"No, he'll be stiff tomorrow, poor old chap," Neil said, starting to groom the grey with a hay wisp. "So'll you, I shouldn't wonder!" he grinned at Michael.

"I daresay I will, my arms ached like anything. How can we cope tomorrow?"

"I can take Sinbad. He hardly did anything today. Could you ride him, Mike? Dad had to go away for a couple of days so he didn't hunt and I'm left with looking after this nag." Neil swept the wisp along the grey's back. "So I'll have to exercise him."

"Lucky you!" said Mandy.

"I'd like to ride him," Michael said, "if you think I could hold him? I don't want to be bolted with again."

"He wouldn't do that, not unless everyone was galloping, which we shan't be doing," Neil assured him. "He only fidgets about and won't stand, he's not hard to ride."

"Okay, that'll be super," Michael said. "Thanks a lot, Neil. We ought to be on watch early. Say three-thirty?"

Mandy groaned. "Goodness! How ghastly!"

"Three's no worse than four if you're getting up

early," Michael said, "and it'll be the last time, with any luck."

"I'll lead Sinbad," said Neil, "and meet you at the usual place—the gate. Can you get Sally there then? We must be dead quiet, keep on the grass all the time. This time we'll *know* that they're there."

"And it'll be jolly dark," Michael said, preparing to mount his bicycle. "It's much darker at four than when we started The Watch. We'll tell Sally the plan on our way back."

"Have you given him a new name?" Mandy asked, looking over the door at the grey. She liked the "stabley" smell and the look of the clean straw. She wished they could keep their ponies up and have rugs for them, (dark blue bound with red and their initials in red) and rollers for the rugs to match, and bandages, and headcollars with white browbands.

"Silver," Neil said, picking up the body brush and rubbing it against the curry comb.

"Jolly nice!"

"Dad's a square over names. He'd go for Prince, or Nobby, or Dandy, but I stuck out for something a bit more zippy!" Neil knocked the curry comb against the wall to clear it of dust.

"Come on, Mandy," Michael said impatiently.

They found Sally helping to feed some calves. She came out into the yard and they told her what they had found out. She stared at them, her eyes round with surprise. "Golly! How simply super!

We'll really get them caught. How marvellous! I was getting a bit fed up with it actually," she confessed, "and so was Mummie."

"So were we," Mandy admitted. "Neil was too."

"But we had to stick it," Michael said seriously. "It's jolly decent of you to have gone on with it, Sally."

"Nice to think this'll be the last time," she said.

"As long as everything comes off all right," said Michael. "Half past three, Sally."

"Okay. I'll be on time. You bet! It'll be most awfully exciting! They'll really be there this time."

Mandy felt a little shiver somewhere round her spine. They'd really be there, in the darkness on the moor—those three men whom she'd said looked horrid. And they would have to get near enough to see exactly what they were doing, and then slip away without being seen or heard.

The twins went home, brought in the ponies and went to bed.

There was no difficulty about getting up next morning, even at three o'clock. As soon as the alarm woke Mandy she remembered everything and thought, This is it! Then she jumped up and began to dress.

Michael was just as quick and they went downstairs together. They drank their milk hurriedly and crammed biscuits into their pockets to eat later (when they remembered them they were too crumbled even for Skipper).

Mandy got Inky and Michael fetched his bicycle.

He had a new battery in the lamp, which was lucky as it was very dark. Chipmunk neighed sadly as they left but Inky didn't answer; they were used to being separated now.

As they came up to the gate they heard the jingle of a bit, and a horse fidgeted, his shoe striking a stone. Inky broke into a jog and Mandy saw a pale shape against the dark of the trees. They found Neil on Silver, he was holding Sinbad's reins. "Hello," she said.

"Good show, you're punctual," Neil said, handing Sinbad's reins to Michael, who had leant his bicycle up against the bank. He mounted and adjusted his stirrup leathers. Then Sally rode up.

"Rather fun, all four of us on watch together!" she said. "Where are we going first?"

"My idea's this—" Neil said, "as there's four of us we can spread out. That way we'll watch a larger bit. Okay?"

"Yep," said Michael keenly.

"We'll be in a line. I'll go at the far end, it's the furthest away and Silver's the fastest—we'll have the longest way to the phone."

"Silver shows up," Mandy said.

"I'll be extra careful to keep out of sight. I'm right along at the far end of the other road, Sally next, just by the ridge we usually stop at, Sally. Mandy where the road meets this bank. You can lurk under the trees on the bank, Mandy. Mike watches the road this end. Okay everyone?"

"Sounds all right," Michael said. "It covers the whole bit, more than we usually manage."

"Do we stand still or ride up and down like sentries?" Sally asked.

"Just as you think. Only don't go too far and leave a big stretch without anybody watching it. Anyway, the lorry must move about so it's sure to come past one of us," Neil said.

"Unless they round up sheep from all over and then drive them to the lorry," Michael said. "We don't know how they do it. Come on," he added impatiently. "Let's get cracking."

"Try not to let a pony neigh," Neil urged. "If you see them make sure they are stealing sheep and go and phone the police. Never mind about the number, it's too difficult to get it. Telling the police is the main thing."

Neil rode along the little path under the bank which they had so often ridden down on dark mornings, and they followed in single file. When they came to where the bank met the road and turned away downhill, Neil stopped and said, "You're here, Mandy. I say, when anyone goes for the police it'd help if he could tell one of us, if we're anywhere near. Then the second chap might manage to get the number."

"Good idea," Michael said, "if we pass one of the Watch. Do let's get on, we're wasting time."

"It's still pitch dark. They won't be hurrying to get away," Neil said. "You go up the road, Mike, as far as you think. Come on, Sally. Dead quiet and keep your eyes skinned!"

Michael had already vanished into the darkness as Sally and Neil rode away leaving Mandy alone. Silver, a pale blurred shape, showed up for two or three minutes and then there was nothing but darkness. Whitesock didn't show up at all, Mandy reflected, and Inky was the blackest and best! She could see his ears against the sky, every now and then he twitched one of them forward or back.

It was a moonless night and rather cold. Mandy felt thankful it was fine, although it was cold, they'd only had to miss watching twice because of rain but it had been drizzling and misty several times. There was not a sound to be heard. How sickening it would be if they didn't come. But I'm sure those men were the rustlers, Mandy thought, so they were probably somewhere out there in the darkness. Or if they came at dawn, as she always imagined they did, they were approaching now, intent on stealing sheep. They wouldn't let anyone stop them, Mandy thought with a little shiver, they'd looked tough.

Inky began to fidget, sidling and tossing his head, so she walked him along beside the road in the direction taken by Michael.

Inky kept breaking into a trot so she let him jog along. After they had gone a little way the road turned sharply and went down hill and Mandy realized she had come further than she had intended. She stopped and listened. It'd be nice to meet Mike but she mustn't leave her bit of moor unguarded. Carefully keeping Inky on the grass beside the road, she turned and started to ride back. There wasn't the faintest glimmer of light yet. It ought to be dawn soon, though the mornings were much later now. Even after all these mornings Mandy enjoyed watching the light grow stronger until the sun came up.

She turned in her saddle and looked towards the east. No sign of it lightening—then she saw a twinkle of light low down. As she watched her heart began to beat a little faster. A light on the moor? It could mean only one thing. The rustlers.

There it was. And a second one. Two little blobs of light moving about, appearing and then disappearing. Mandy was puzzled. Then she thought, They're working with torches, not the lorry's lights. P'r'aps the lorry isn't there. I wonder if Mike's seen them?

She must make sure that it was *them*. And that they really were stealing sheep. She tried to think whereabouts the men were. The road turned and twisted a good deal but it didn't go over there. The grass track below their Secret Coombe—that's where they were. Mike wouldn't see them from where he was. It was up to her.

Mandy's heart was thumping uncomfortably as she turned and rode towards the lights bobbing about on the moor.

CHAPTER ELEVEN

MANDY AND INKY

It was still quite dark on the moor which was a good thing. The men taking sheep would show up in the light from their torches, Mandy thought, so she wouldn't have to go very close. Just watch while they caught one sheep and then hurry to the telephone in the village. She'd thought it all out so often, what she'd do when the rustlers came, but now it was really happening it didn't seem so easy. For one thing, Inky wasn't good at going over rough ground in the dark. The moor was seldom level, only on the grass tracks, among the heather there were little banks, dips and holes. Even in daylight Inky went unwillingly.

If only she was riding Chipmunk or Whitesock, thought Mandy as she urged him on. When he stopped she had to use her heels vigorously and it was surprising what a noise it seemed to make, the saddle flaps sounded like slapping and the bit jingled when Inky tossed his head.

The lights had disappeared. Behind clumps of gorse? Or was there a little hill between her and them? She wasn't sure how far away they were. Then the lights shone out again, much nearer than she had expected and she stopped in a fright.

They were being very quiet. Mandy was surprised not to hear the dog bark, sheep dogs generally did, but perhaps they'd trained him not to. A beam of light swung across the heather, there was a startled bleat and Mandy had a glimpse of a man holding a sheep. Inky snorted and she whispered "It's all right, Inky boy," and stroked him. They *were* the sheep rustlers. Now she must give the alarm.

Quietly though, she was too near them to take any risks. It would be dreadful if they knew they'd been seen and got away before the police could come. Specially as she hadn't taken their number. She turned Inky, he was anxious to go back for ponies sense anything strange or dangerous, and she began to ride back towards the road.

She went slowly. Once they reached the road she could trot along on the grass beside it. And as soon as she was further away she could trot along the road which would be quicker. Not too soon though, for sound carries a long way at night.

She wondered how many sheep they'd caught. Those were Daddy's probably. She'd imagined they rounded up a bunch of sheep, with sheep dogs, and drove them into a lorry but they were catching them as they slept. It was a quieter way and men used to handling sheep could do it quickly. Mandy had watched sheep being caught and dipped in water (to prevent disease) and she'd seen how easily it was done by skilled men.

Inky stopped, jibbing at a steep little bank with

a ditch beyond it. Mandy persuaded him to go down it slowly and carefully. On the far side she saw the road just in front of them. Good! Now she could trot. She touched Inky with her heels and he went on willingly. Mandy's spirits rose. The rustlers would be caught and everything would be all right.

It had not begun to get light yet and the road was distinguishable because it was lighter than the grass beside it, on which Mandy was riding.

They seemed to strike a rough patch of ground. Inky stumbled and Mandy held him up "Steady boy!" He went on for a pace or two and then came to a limping halt.

Mandy jumped off. Her heart felt like lead. Not lame. He couldn't be lame. His leg—the vet had said if it went again he was finished.

"Inky!" He stood stock still. She tried to coax him forward to see how bad he was but he wouldn't move. She tugged at the reins. "Come on, Inky, just a little way." He hobbled for a step or two and stopped. Even in the dark Mandy knew he was dead lame in a hind leg.

What on earth could she do? Alone on the moor in the dark with a lame pony. If only Mike were here! He'd know what to do. He'd said they ought to go in pairs as one alone could get in a jam. Mandy felt desperately lonely for her twin.

Surely a vet could cure Inky, even if it took ages. She put her cheek against his neck. "I'll get you sound again somehow, Inky." She wasn't going to admit, even to herself, that he might have to be put to sleep. She blinked hard to get rid of the tears that kept coming.

The rustlers! She'd forgotten them in her misery. She was the only person who knew where they were. She *must* get to the telephone although it meant leaving Inky. He couldn't go far so there was no worry about catching him again. The rustlers might come past but luckily he was some yards from the road, they wouldn't run into him and nobody would steal a pony that was dead lame.

Better take off his tack, they'd think he was a moor pony. As long as they didn't hurt him . . . Mandy clenched her teeth. It was dreadful to leave him but she must. She pushed the saddle and bridle into a big clump of heather, gave Inky a last pat and a kiss on his nose, and then she ran down the road towards Willacombe.

She was soon out of breath and had to walk. Running and walking alternately she hurried on, trying to keep back her tears. She mustn't think about Inky.

But her thoughts kept coming back to him. They'd get him home to Pippacotts and she'd look after him and let him rest his leg. How did you move a pony as lame as that? He couldn't walk at all.

Daddy would know. Perhaps he could be got into a cattle lorry. That reminded her of the rustlers and she began to run again.

It was beginning to get lighter. The sky was a paler grey and the moor no longer looked like a black sea. Had she really come as far along the road as this? It seemed miles to go back. There was a loop in the road here and if she cut across it she'd save a few minutes.

She left the road and plunged into the heather. A few steps and she knew she'd made a mistake, for it was much slower pushing through the knee-high heather and stumbling over uneven ground than running along a road. Especially as it was still dark.

Mandy blundered on, she thought it would be quicker than going back for the road couldn't be far ahead. A few minutes later she was still wading through heather and wasting precious time. Surely she ought to have come out on the road by now?

She stopped. Mike had said that you went round in a circle if you couldn't see. Suppose she hadn't kept straight—when she came out on a road she wouldn't know if she'd crossed the short cut or gone back to where she'd left the road. Bother the darkness! If only Mike were here.

Undecided, she stood still. It would be the same road so it wouldn't matter awfully, except for wasted time. So long as she went the right way and not back to where she'd left Inky. She took a step forward and stopped for she had heard something brushing through the heather.

A pony's head appeared outlined against the sky, it came nearer and she saw the rider dimly. "Mike! Oh, Mike, I'm so glad you're here."

"Mandy—where's Inky?"

"He's lame. I had to leave him," Mandy sobbed. "The rustlers are just over there. I saw them catch a sheep."

"Gosh! We'll get them in the bag!"

"Can you go and telephone?" Mandy was standing with her hand on Sinbad's neck. Michael was leaning forward to talk to her. It was comforting to have him there.

"Yep. But what happened to Inky?"

"He sort of stumbled. I can't think why as we were by the road not out on the moor and it seemed quite flat. Anyway, I couldn't see. He's dead lame in his hind leg."

"Oh gosh! What rotten luck," Michael said sympathetically. "Perhaps it won't be all that bad."

Mandy mopped her eyes and sniffed. "P'r'aps the vet could cure him," she said but without much hope. "Mike, we must tell the police about the rustlers. If they aren't caught everything's wasted." (And Inky needn't have gone lame, she thought.) "Why did you come over here? It's not in your bit of patrol."

"I thought you wanted me," Michael said simply.

"I'm glad you did. You *must* go and phone."

"Okay. Sinbad's smashing to ride."

"I'll go and stay with Inky."

"I'll be back soon." Michael touched Sinbad with his heels and the chestnut rocketed forward. "Steady, you ass!"

"Where's the road?" Mandy called.

"Dead behind you or bang ahead!" Michael disappeared into the darkness.

So I did keep straight, Mandy thought and started to walk back. Now I've got to find Inky. She came to the road and trudged along it. Everything was always further than you thought it was. Seeing Michael had cheered her up and she didn't feel lonely now.

She found Inky standing where she'd left him. As she came up to him he threw up his head, ears pricked, and when she said, "Inky boy," he put his head down and nuzzled her sleeve. Mandy hugged his neck. "Darling Inky. You've got to get all right." Then she stood by him and rubbed his head behind his ears, he always liked this.

Suddenly he threw up his head again and pricked his ears, just as he'd done when he heard her coming. Mandy listened. She couldn't hear anything. "What is it, Inky? What can you hear?"

She listened again. This time she heard a steady thudding on the grass, it was coming nearer, then a dark form loomed up and stopped beside her. Mandy smelt the nice smell of warm pony as Sally's voice said, "Mandy."

"Sally! How did you know?"

"I met Mike. I got bored with standing about and nothing happening so I rode towards where you were. I met Mike dashing off to the phone. I am sorry, Mandy. Is he awfully lame?"

"Dead lame. He can't even hobble. I can't

think what did it. The ground was flat and he didn't twist or anything."

"Where are the rustlers? Did you see them?"

"They rustled a sheep. I saw them rustling," Mandy said proudly. "They're down there. They were nearer when I first saw them. They must've got their lorry on the grass track below Secret Coombe. Look, there's a light. They must be working round in a big circle picking up sheep and lugging them to the lorry. They're awfully quiet but sometimes you hear a sheep baa."

If only they had the lorry's number. Mandy looked where the lights were like pin points. Those three men were there, and their dog. It was still rather dark. Could they get near enough to see the number without being seen themselves?

"If we could get the lorry's number it'd make certain of catching them," she said. "Dare we?"

"We'd have to go quite close," Sally said doubtfully. "But it's fairly dark still. I suppose we ought to, just to make sure they're caught. But I don't much want to."

"Nor do I," Mandy admitted. "But I think it's jolly important. You stay here, Sally. It's not your show."

"Not much. I'd be scared alone. I'm coming."

"Thanks," Mandy said. "Let's get it over."

Sally unsaddled Whitesock and left him with Inky. Then she followed Mandy.

CHAPTER TWELVE

A DESPERATE CHASE

As they began to move slowly down the slope Mandy thought it was rather a relief to be doing something. Anything was better than standing about waiting—and thinking about Inky.

"They'll be going soon I expect," Sally said, "as it's getting lighter." She looked at her watch. "It's just after five. Seems ages since we got up and came out."

"I don't believe we've been coming out early enough," Mandy said. "They work in the dark, not at dawn as we thought. It doesn't matter as nobody's lost any sheep so we've not missed seeing them."

"We'd have been here by the time they left," Sally said. "They must've got the lorry full by now."

"I suppose each sheep takes quite a time to find, and to catch and then to get into the lorry," Mandy said.

She was keeping her eyes on the lights bobbing about below them. Sometimes one light, sometimes two or three, they appeared and vanished, flashed across the ground or shone steadily in one place.

As they came nearer they caught the sound of men's voices from time to time and some indignant bleating, but the rustlers were making very little noise. Not that there's ever anyone out here to hear them, Mandy thought.

They halted in the cover of a tall clump of heather.

"It's getting awfully light," Mandy said in a low voice. She didn't want to go any nearer but she felt they must get the lorry's number or all their watching might be wasted. She clenched her teeth and made up her mind not to show that she was frightened. It was jolly decent of Sally to stick to her. "Come on," she said resolutely. "If we're not quick it'll be light."

They crawled for a short distance through pricking heather growing in dusty dark earth. As they worked their way down the hill bracken took the place of heather. It was tall and had rather a nice smell. Mandy was worried by the way it rustled and waved about as they crawled through it, and the stems were bare which meant they weren't at all well hidden. It ended suddenly and when Mandy stopped Sally bumped into her.

"Look out," Mandy hissed and Sally crawled up beside her. They parted the stems and peeped through them.

"There's the lorry," Mandy whispered. "It's just like the one Mike and I saw. I bet it is the same one. I never thought of taking the number—

anyway, we'd have to go near enough to make sure it's the same lorry."

"How are we going to get close enough?" Sally asked.

Mandy looked at the stretch of grass ahead. How *were* they going to cross it without being seen? She looked to the left where the bare grass stretched away up the hill, no use that way. Downhill, on their right, the bracken was high and thick and it grew in a long curve which ended quite close to where the lorry stood.

"That way," Mandy whispered. "It won't be difficult to keep hidden. Only I wish the bracken grew further apart so we could crawl through it without touching the stems, they may see it moving."

Sally began to say they wouldn't see it move in the dark and then stopped, because it wasn't really dark any more.

They moved down the hill slowly and carefully but the bracken rustled and swayed above their heads, and sometimes a dead stem snapped. They were making too much noise, Mandy thought, and she stopped.

Peering through the bracken stalks she saw, in the grey light, that two men were standing by the lorry. She couldn't see them distinctly enough to tell if they were the men who'd been with the lorry in the field yesterday—and there'd been three men.

Now they were so close they'd have to be extra

careful not to make any noise. Rather frightening to be so near those rustlers but they couldn't give up and go back without the lorry's number.

She began to crawl forward, stopping every few yards to look towards the men by the lorry. They were standing talking, she could hear their voices though not what they said. One of them lit a cigarette, Mandy could see the match flare and then she forced herself to go on. Sally was close at her heels and Mandy found this comforting, she'd have been much more frightened if she'd been alone.

They came to the end of the bracken and only a patch of short grass lay between them and the men by the lorry. Now it was almost light. A tiny bit nearer and she'd be able to read the number. She looked round and saw a narrow strip of bracken sticking out towards the lorry, not wide enough for more than one person to hide there and they might see her through the bare stalks but if she was going to get that number she must take a chance. Dare she? She bit her lip and made up her mind. She wouldn't funk it, she'd go nearer.

"Wait here," she whispered to Sally.

Then she wriggled forward, inch by inch. Her heart was thumping and she clenched her teeth. She wouldn't think about the rustlers seeing her, just keep her mind on getting the lorry's number.

Now she'd reached the end of the strip of bracken. She sank down, her arms ached from crawling and something sharp was sticking into her knee, but she could read the lorry's number. She said it to herself several times to learn it thoroughly. Then she began to wriggle back to where Sally was waiting. She had nearly reached Sally when a dead stick cracked loudly under her weight. Mandy froze to a statue-like stillness and held her breath. "If only it was still dark. Wish I wasn't wearing this red jersey. Lucky that dog we saw isn't here!"

A man's voice shouted, "Someone in that bracken, watchin' us. Cor, wait till I get my 'ands on 'im." Looking up, Mandy saw one of the men coming towards her.

She jumped up. "Run, Sally. It's okay, I've got their number."

As she turned and ran after Sally she wished she hadn't said that, the man had been near enough to have heard and it would make him keen to catch them. They were in an awful jam. They fled up the hill, running as fast as they could.

It was hard work running through long grass and heather and they had to go round patches of bracken. Looking back over her shoulder Mandy saw that both men were running after them and one of them was gaining on them. He called something but she couldn't hear what he said. He was going to catch them very soon.

He couldn't do anything to them, Mandy told herself, but he was going to be very angry with them for spying on him. Thieves were pretty rough people.

If only there was somewhere they could hide.

Secret Coombe!

Mandy swerved towards it. "This way. Our coombe." Sally was beside her and they were running across the hill now, instead of upwards and it was much easier. But of course it was easier for the man chasing them too.

Mandy was beginning to get out of breath but she kept on running. Very soon they'd start to go downhill and then they'd come to the long narrow gully leading into Secret Coombe.

He'd see them go in but once inside he'd never find them. There were lots of good hiding places in Secret Coombe. The deep hollow behind a big rock that was almost as good as a cave, the dell full of thick, low bushes—she and Mike had made tunnels through them—and the rocky ledge at the top end, high up and hidden by ferns. Inside Secret Coombe they could hide where nobody would find them.

A loud shout came from their pursuer and Mandy thought he must see they were going to get away and he was cross. The shout was followed by a long shrill whistle, the kind of whistle a shepherd uses to direct his dog when he's far up on a hill. Mandy thought she heard another whistle, further away, but she didn't take any notice because escaping was what mattered.

They began to go down towards the long narrow gully.

"Nearly there," Mandy panted breathlessly, as

they slithered down the steep side to the bottom of the ravine. The stream from Secret Coombe ran down it and left little room so that Mandy and Sally ran beside it, jumping on and off stones and sometimes splashing into the water.

The entrance to Secret Coombe was just ahead and once they'd slipped between the trees they'd be safe.

A stone came hurtling down beside them. Mandy looked up and saw a man coming down, scattering stones and loose earth, behind him Mandy saw a dog. He was the third man and it must have been to him that their pursuer had shouted and whistled, and his answering whistle that she'd heard.

"We'll just make it," she said.

"Hurry," gasped Sally.

They heard him crashing down the steep side of the little valley and then a splash told them that he'd reached the stream. Mandy had a quick look back and saw that he'd fallen but was getting to his feet.

Then they dived into the cover of the trees, slipping between the trunks and ducking under low branches. The tree tops met and shut out the sky. It was green and dim and cool. The ground was soft and damp and in places there were big rocks. The stream rippled over stones and widened out into little pools. It was very quiet. Mandy led the way up the little glen. She knew where they could hide safely, with no fear of being found, until they heard the lorry drive away.

"Don't make such a row," Mandy said in a low voice, as Sally tripped over a long bramble spray and stumbled into a bush which rustled loudly.

"Sorry," Sally muttered. "But I don't think he's coming after us now."

Mandy stopped for a second to listen. There was no sound of pursuit and she said thankfully, "He's given up. But we'd better be awfully quiet in case he's near."

They went on slowly, avoiding dead sticks which would crack, and stopping boughs from springing back noisily. They had nearly reached the end of the coombe when Sally gripped Mandy's arm. "He's coming," she whispered.

There was a rustling of leaves from the lower end of the coombe, and the scrape of a heavy boot on a rock.

"Quick, we're nearly there," Mandy said, moving forward. "Be jolly quiet."

She led the way through some tall bracken and then scrambled on to a big rock beside the stream, where it splashed over some boulders in a little waterfall. Above them there was a wall of rock with ferns growing out of it.

"There's a ledge up here," Mandy said. "I'll go first and show you. Be careful not to bash the ferns."

She began to pull herself up. Sally climbed up after her and found herself on a shelf of rock just wide enough for them both.

"Marvellous!" she whispered. "He'll never find us here."

"Sh —" Mandy whispered. "He's coming."

They crouched side by side and listened to the rustling and crackling sounds coming nearer. Mandy tried to smile encouragingly at Sally but it wasn't easy. Of course they were perfectly safe, hidden so well, but it was very frightening, all the same, hearing the rustler coming so close.

Then the man spoke and Mandy went cold with fear.

"Good dog," he said, "seek 'em, good dog."

She'd forgotten the dog. It would follow them by scent and they'd be trapped.

"The dog will find us," she breathed in Sally's ear. "We must get away."

"Where?" Sally looked round wildly.

There wasn't time to get down and go on up the coombe. Could they climb up any further? They had to, there was nowhere else to go. Mandy stood up and looked at the rock behind them. It wasn't very high and beyond it was the side of the coombe which went up to the moor. Crashing sounds below them decided her. "Come on, Sally, up here."

A bush hung down over the rock and Mandy grasped one of its boughs and began to pull herself up, feeling for little ledges with her feet and shifting her hands higher, one at a time, as she climbed. If the branch broke or the bush pulled out of the ground she'd crash, but she reached the top of the rock and got her knee up on to it. She lay sprawling for a second and then swung round to help Sally who had begun to climb. Mandy leaned down to give her a hand and Sally, who was light and quick, joined her on the big flat rock.

They both knelt, silent and listening, and they could hear the man pushing through the bushes below them. The dog gave a little whimper and Mandy shivered. It was horrid feeling that they were being hunted.

"Come on," she whispered and they began to work their way up towards the moor.

It was very difficult because of having to move very quietly, and also because the hillside was so steep. The earth slipped away from under their feet, they clung to little bushes which broke, or whipped back against their faces, and they were scratched by brambles. It was lucky, Mandy thought, that the man was making a good deal of noise himself or he'd hear them.

Just before they reached the top they came to a big patch of gorse bushes and they had to work their way round it. Loose earth crumbled and filled their shoes and little stones went rolling down the coombe side.

"He'll hear us," Sally said.

They stopped on the edge of the coombe, still hidden but with the open moor in front of them. They listened, glad of a minute's rest, and they were relieved not to hear anything.

"He's given up. Thank goodness!" said Mandy.

CHAPTER THIRTEEN

INKY'S LAMENESS

"WHERE shall we go now?" Sally asked.

Mandy looked at the moor and thought it was very bare. She didn't like the thought of leaving the shelter of Secret Coombe but it wasn't safe to stay—not with that dog on their scent.

"We must keep out of sight till the lorry's gone," she replied. "We'll hear it go. If we could get up to the road we could hide in all that tall heather where the ponies are, then we'd see the lorry go. If Inky wasn't lame we'd be okay to ride away."

"We can creep along through the bracken," Sally said. "And keep a bit of a hill between us and where the lorry is."

"They'll be leaving any time now and we'll hear the lorry's engine start and can hide," Mandy said.

They left the cover of Secret Coombe and set out across the moor, they were making for a fold in the hill which went up towards the road and where they would be hidden as they went up the hillside.

"We were jolly lucky to get away," Sally was saying and then she stopped dead. "Mandy, look—" she whispered. "It's them."

Mandy stared and saw the two rustlers they'd thought were at the lorry. She felt an odd tingling down her spine, her knees trembled and she bit her lip to stop herself shivering. To have got away and then to run straight into them again.

Mandy stood with Sally clutching her arm. They hadn't been seen yet but they were caught on a patch of grass with no cover near.

"Go back?" Sally whispered.

"The dog'd find us," Mandy answered under her breath. "Keep absolutely still and they mayn't see us."

They stood, hardly daring to breathe, for the rustlers were quite close and were walking back towards the lorry.

It was going to be all right, they were walking away—then Mandy heard a sound she was dreading. A crashing through the bushes behind them as the third rustler came out of Secret Coombe. The two men turned to see and they noticed the girls.

"There they are, them little snoopers," one of them exclaimed. "They took our number."

"Run," Mandy said wildly and they started up the bare moor with no hiding place in sight. They'd never get away this time, Mandy thought. She ran her hardest but they were tired after so much running, and she felt despairing for they'd never get away.

Then Sally exclaimed, "The boys. Up there."

Mandy looked up the hill towards the road and

saw two horses on the skyline. Silver and Sinbad. As she looked they moved downhill towards the running girls.

Neil was waving and he shouted something Mandy couldn't hear clearly and Michael called, "Okay, we're coming."

Mandy and Sally put on a spurt as they ran. Once they'd joined up with the boys there'd be four of them and Neil would think of some way of getting rid of the rustlers.

The men behind them were calling out, and they heard that shrill whistle again. Mandy looked round. "The dog," she exclaimed. "He's sending it after us."

"The mean thing!" Sally said disgustedly.

They ran on but Mandy kept looking back anxiously. The dog, a big sheep dog, was coming after them fast and silently.

Mandy guessed it would do the one thing it had been trained to do—round them up as if they were sheep. As long as they stood still and kept together it would stand and watch them. If they tried to get away it would nip their legs. It'd mean the rustlers could stop them getting away, even with the boys there.

Neil saw what was going to happen—he'd often helped his father work sheep with a dog—and he hurried Silver along. They thundered up to Mandy and Sally, and Neil yelled, "Okay, we'll help."

"Reinforcements!" shouted Michael, who was enjoying himself terrifically.

They pulled up beside the girls. Neil had a riding crop with a long thong and he swung it, making Sinbad plunge about, but keeping the dog at a distance.

"Get up behind us," Neil said hurriedly. "Buck up or those chaps'll be here. Mandy on Sinbad, it's okay, he's done it before. Come on, Sally. Put your foot on mine and give me your hand. I'll heave you up."

"I can't reach your foot," Sally gasped. She was breathless from running and she had a stitch in her side.

"Get on that hilly bit," Neil directed, turning Silver so that he was on lower ground than Sally. "Hurry, those blokes are coming and they look pretty mad with us."

Mandy was finding it easier to get on Sinbad as he was not nearly as tall as Silver. He stood still, which was surprising, and putting her foot on Michael's, and grasping his hand, she managed to scramble up behind him.

It felt very peculiar to be behind the saddle instead of on it and she felt most insecure.

"Hang on to me," Michael ordered and Mandy put her arms round her twin's waist.

"If one of us falls off we'll both go," she said.

Sally was mounted behind Neil and was clinging to him. The men had almost reached them, another minute and they would have been caught by them. They looked very cross.

Neil said, "Hang on, Sally. Get going, Mike."

He touched Silver with his heels and the big grey went straight into an easy slow canter.

Sinbad lunged forward nearly unseating Mandy but she hung on and Michael steadied the chestnut who settled down to canter beside Silver.

"Just in the nick of time," said Neil.

"Yes," Mandy said. "Thanks awfully for coming to the rescue." She tried to look back but Michael said she'd have them both off if she didn't keep still.

"What made them chase you?" Neil asked. "How did they come to find you?"

"We went quite close so as to get the lorry's number," Mandy explained. "They saw us and I called to Sally that I'd got the number. They heard and that made them chase us. We hid in Secret Coombe but the man with the dog came after us. I was awfully scared."

"What would they have done if they'd caught us?" Sally wondered.

"Threatened you to make you promise not to tell anyone about them," Neil said. "Jolly good show your getting the number. The police asked if I knew it when I rang them. I'll belt off and ring them again. They'll get the rustlers for certain. They'll be zooming after 'em in police cars. Wish I was with them."

"Listen," said Michael, pulling up. "That's the lorry."

They could hear it grinding along in low gear. Neil stood up in his stirrups to try and see.

"Don't," begged Sally. "Keep still so I can hold on to you. I'm terribly wobbly and the ground looks miles away from up here."

"There it is," exclaimed Michael. They looked where he was pointing and saw the lorry moving slowly along the track. It disappeared behind a rise in the ground and then reappeared higher up. Reaching the road, it turned, increased its speed and went out of sight.

"They'll soon be stopped," Neil said confidently.

They went on towards the road. It was awfully difficult not to bump about, Mandy found, she was sitting too far back to be able to grip with her knees. Silver was just ahead and she could see Sally was having an easier ride for he had a lovely smooth canter.

"Sinbad's jolly good," she said, "to let us do this."

"He's done it before," Neil explained, "with a cousin I had to stay last hols. What's this about Inky? Is he badly lamed? I met Mike and came along with him and he told me."

"I'm afraid he is," Mandy said sadly. "It was pitch dark so I couldn't see a thing—I haven't a clue what made him stumble—but he can't even hobble."

"Bad luck," Neil said. "But a vet may get him right."

"What are we going to do about getting him back to Pippacotts?" Michael asked.

"That's what's worrying me," said Mandy. Hiring a lorry would be expensive, and there'd be the vet's bill. She had a little money in the Post Office Savings Bank but not much and she didn't think she could ask her father to pay. He was hard up and he'd lost a lot of sheep.

"Dad's got a horse trailer that he sticks on behind the Land-Rover," Neil said. "I'm sure he'd come along and pick up Inky. Only we'll have to wait till he comes home tonight."

"Would he really? That'd be marvellous," Mandy said gratefully. "I'll stay with Inky all day. We'll have to bring him water. And hay as he can't move to graze."

"He's as lame as that, is he?" Neil asked. "A bad show."

"I'll bring everything up on my bike," Michael said. "And food for us."

"Thanks," Mandy said. It wouldn't be so bad staying there all day if Mike was with her.

"There he is," said Sally. "And Whitesock's just beside him. I hope I can catch him."

"He'll come up to the others, I expect," said Mandy.

Inky whinnied with pleasure as they rode up. Mandy and Sally dismounted and Mandy went to Inky and patted him.

Neil put his reins over Silver's head and asked Michael to hold them. Michael didn't answer. He was looking at Inky in a puzzled way.

"Mandy," he exclaimed. "It's his other leg.

He's resting his off hind. His weak leg's the near hind."

"*Oh!*" Mandy went quite white with excitement. "Then perhaps —."

"Let's have a look. Hang on for a minute, Mike." Neil gave him Silver's reins and then went up to Inky.

First he patted him and stroked his nose, then he ran his hand along his back and down his hind quarter to his fetlock, which he held firmly. "Come up, old boy." Inky picked up his foot.

"*Well*," Neil exclaimed.

"What is it?" Michael asked.

Mandy and Sally were hanging over Neil as he bent down holding Inky's foot.

Mandy stood up. Her eyes were shining. "A stone. That's all. He's picked up a stone."

"We'll soon have it out," Neil said.

"What with?" Michael asked. "We haven't got a knife with one of those things in it."

"The end of my crop." Neil had tucked his riding crop under his stirrup leather. He fetched it and proceeded to lever out the stone, using the crook at the end of the crop. Inky put his foot down and stood on it. Neil held up the stone. "That's it."

"He's standing on it properly. He's okay," Mandy cried. "Thanks awfully, Neil." She hugged Inky's neck and felt almost like bursting into tears.

"Just lead him on, to make sure," Neil advised.

She led him forward. "He's sound. I can hardly believe it."

"Thank goodness," said Michael.

They caught Whitesock without any trouble and Sally mounted him.

"I'm going on as fast as I can," Neil told them. "So as to give the police the number. What is it, Mandy?"

She told him and he went off at a canter along the grass at the roadside. The others followed him, jogging along slowly until they came to the gate where they had met on so many mornings to start their watch. Michael's bicycle was where he had left it, propped against a bank.

"I've got to get Sinbad back," he said. "What a bore! I'll have to walk."

"If you lead Inky I'll ride your bike then we can come back together," Mandy suggested.

They did this and as they were saying goodbye to Sally at the Southcott turning, they heard a horse on the road and Silver came into sight.

"I came back for Sinbad," Neil said. "I rang the police and they sounded as if they were certain to get the lorry now they know the number. Smashing we caught them!"

He took Sinbad and the twins returned to Pippacotts, turning out Inky as they passed the paddock. Pippacotts looked very nice in the early sunshine, with its white walls and thatched roof and Mrs. Foster's bed of red and yellow flowers. Skipper greeted them and the latest batch of kittens was playing round the back door, while their mother lapped milk from a saucer. Now they'd stay here for ever, Mandy thought hopefully.

Mr. Foster came out of the barn and Michael shouted, "Daddy, we caught the rustlers. The police are after them."

"We got their lorry's number and Neil phoned it to the police," Mandy said.

Mr. Foster stared at them in astonishment. "Really? I never thought you would. That's wonderful!"

"They'll catch them as they've got the number," Michael said. "Mandy and Sally got it."

"They're sure to catch them, then," Mr. Foster said. "You've done a great job with your Pony Watch. It'll stop the rustling. If it should start up again I'll organise a watch myself, now you've shown it can be done."

"We won't have to leave Pippacotts?" Mandy asked.

"Not if the rustling's stopped. We'll manage now. And when I sell this year's wool I'll buy a couple of Exmoor ponies, little mares to start our herd."

"Oh, Daddy, how super!" Mandy said.

"You'll have to look after them," he told the twins.

"Oh, we will. Super!"

"You've earned a reward for all that watching you did, and all those mornings you turned out so early."

"It was well worth it," said Michael, "as we copped 'em."

"Pippacotts and ponies," sighed Mandy. "Bliss!"